HADASSAH

Hadassah

AN AMERICAN STORY

Hadassah Lieberman

Brandeis University Press   Waltham, Massachusetts

Brandeis University Press
© 2021 Hadassah Lieberman
All rights reserved
Manufactured in the United States of America
Designed by Mindy Basinger Hill
Typeset in Parkinson Electra Pro

For permission to reproduce any of the material in this book,
contact Brandeis University Press, 415 South Street,
Waltham MA 02453, or visit brandeis.edu/press.

Library of Congress Cataloging-in-Publication Data

Names: Lieberman, Hadassah, author.

Title: Hadassah : an American story / Hadassah Lieberman.

Description: First edition. | Waltham, Massachusetts : Brandeis
University Press, [2021] | Series: HBI series on Jewish women | *Summary*:
"Hadassah Lieberman's memoirs, telling the story of her experience
as the child of Holocaust survivors, of being an immigrant in America,
making a career as a working woman, experiencing divorce, and
re-marriage as the wife of a US senator"— Provided by publisher.

Identifiers: LCCN 2020047044 (print) | LCCN 2020047045 (ebook) |
ISBN 9781684580378 (hardcover) | ISBN 9781684580385 (ebook)

Subjects: LCSH: Lieberman, Hadassah. | Vice-Presidential candidates'
spouses—United States—Biography. | Jewish women—United States—
Biography. | Jews—United States—Biography.

Classification: LCC E184.37.L53 A3 2021 (print) |
LCC E184.37.L53 (ebook) | DDC 305.48/8924—dc23

LC record available at https://lccn.loc.gov/2020047044
LC ebook record available at https://lccn.loc.gov/2020047045

5   4   3   2   1

I believe firmly and profoundly that whoever listens
to a witness becomes a witness, so those who hear us,
those who read us must continue to bear witness for us.
Until now, they're doing it with us. At a certain
point in time, they will do it for all of us.

ELIE WIESEL

Contents

Illustrations follow page 72

List of Illustrations

Foreword

I am not unbiased about the author of this book.

On April 11, 1982, I drove from New Haven, Connecticut, to Riverdale, New York, to meet Hadassah, and I immediately fell in love with her. We were married less than a year later on March 20, 1983, in my hometown of Stamford, Connecticut. She has been my indispensable partner in life since that day. I can gratefully say I am even more in love with her than I was on the day we met.

Hadassah Freilich Lieberman is a gifted, good, and gracious person. She had an impressive professional life in the pharmaceutical industry until she married me, and, as we joke, I ruined her career. In fact, she continued to work part-time throughout my six years as Connecticut's attorney general and twenty-four years in the US Senate—first at a Catholic hospital in New Haven, then at two health care consulting firms in Washington, DC, and the Susan G. Komen Race for the Cure for Breast Cancer.

In the midst of all that, she blended our four children into one family. As Hadassah says, we are both parents of all four, even though neither of us is the biological parent of all of them. And now she is the devoted and loving *Savta* (Hebrew for Grandma) to our twelve grandchildren.

This book is Hadassah's extraordinary life story. It goes from her birth in Prague, Czechoslovakia, to parents who survived the Nazi Holocaust; to her childhood far away from Europe as the daughter of a rabbi in a small New England city, Gardner, Massachusetts; to her professional career in the pharmaceutical industry; to becoming my partner in our private and public lives; to her emergence as a national figure in her own right during our 2000 vice-presidential campaign.

The arc of Hadassah's life is a miraculous journey from the horrors of the Holocaust to the heights of American society. It is a story of survival and strength, inspiration and hope, and it will remind you, the reader, of the blessings of freedom and opportunity America gives to its citizens.

For me, Hadassah has provided unwavering love and support and the best and most honest counsel I could want. I could not have achieved whatever I have without her. Living with Hadassah has taught me a lot about life, especially about being the child of survivors and an immigrant to America.

Growing up Jewish in America after World War II, I was certainly aware of the Holocaust, but all my family had left Europe for the United States and Israel before the war. Marrying Hadassah brought me into the lives of her parents—her father a survivor of Nazi slave labor camps in Hungary, her mother a survivor of the Auschwitz and Dachau concentration camps. As Hadassah describes them in the pages of this story, her parents were amazingly resilient. They pressed forward proudly after the war to build a life and family for themselves, first in Prague and then, after the Communists seized control of Czechoslovakia, in America. But they were forever scarred and shaped by the Holocaust, and so too was their daughter, and so too, through our marriage, was I.

Hadassah and her family brought me personally into the nightmarish Holocaust experience and all it teaches about human nature and the capacity of leaders and governments to do good and evil. It influenced my worldview and helped shape the policies I pursued in my public life, particularly in advancing the rule of law and human rights here at home and around the rest of the world, and supporting strong and realistic American foreign and defense policies.

I was born in America to parents who were also born in America, but all four of my grandparents were immigrants, and one of them—my mother's mother—lived with us during most of my childhood and was like a third parent to me. In other words, I was not as personally distant from the immigrant experience as I was from the Holocaust experience before I met and married Hadassah. But, still, she and her parents were themselves immigrants, and that defined Hadassah and still does. She has great appreciation for the opportunities America gave her family, which native-born Americans too often don't have. But she also remembers the difficulties and challenges they confronted as immigrants and the ways in which she was expected to help her parents work their way into and through life in America. The fact that her parents were immigrants has been a great motivator for Hadassah to work hard to succeed and, as her father would say, to "write your name in the sky." During our 2000 national campaign, she did in fact write her name in the sky. I will never forget that night at the Democratic National Convention when Hadassah introduced me to accept the vice-presidential nomination and the delegates were holding thousands of signs with one word on them: "Hadassah." During the campaign, she reached out to immigrants all over America from all over the world, and they warmly responded to and embraced her as one of their own.

Hadassah and I will always do all that we can to welcome and support new immigrants as our families were welcomed and supported by those who came to America before us.

I am very proud that my wife has written her story in this book and grateful that the distinguished Brandeis University Press is publishing it.

I know that in the pages ahead, you will learn a lot about Hadassah (maybe about me too) that you did not know before, and I know that you will enjoy and benefit from the words she has written.

Joseph Lieberman

Preface

Why have I decided to write this book? Why does anyone who has led what she believes is an interesting life want to share her insights, challenges, and lessons learned? Certainly, to help others and to give back. At the same time, there is perhaps a selfish reason: the telling provides a benefit to the teller. By choosing to put your life on display in this way, you are able to gain perspective and then move forward.

In some ways, my story is not unique. Like many other Americans, I am an immigrant—in my case, born in Prague, to two Holocaust survivors—and grew up a naturalized citizen in a small town in New England. A part of the workforce for decades, I've been married, divorced, and remarried. I'm a mother to both my biological and nonbiological children, and a grandmother. But I've also been privileged—and challenged—to be in the public eye as the wife of a prominent public servant, perhaps the role for which I am best known.

Recently I had the opportunity to visit the National World War II Museum in New Orleans. The exhibit underscores the impact the war had on everyone's lives, from the men and women in uniform to the families back home. Defeating the Nazis was truly a collective effort for our country and our allies. As part of the unfolding war narrative, the exhibit presents a massive color-coded map: red for the territories controlled by the Axis powers and blue for the Allies.

Witnessing the huge areas of red threatening to swallow up the entire map was alarming. Though this is a history that is familiar to me, it was distressing to see this visual about the anti-Semitism and hate propagated by the Third Reich and ponder how this evil might have enveloped the globe.

Like other children of Holocaust survivors, I grew up in the shadow of that evil—all the more reason why it's difficult to hear the anti-Semitic language being used currently in some quarters and magnified by the Internet, which contains the same vitriol and loathing of the "other" found in Nazi propaganda. Have we learned nothing from the past? I hope that my own story will serve as a reminder of the values inherent in our democracy and the need for greater tolerance and understanding rather than antipathy.

In this book, I have included the observations and recollections of some relatives, close friends, and colleagues. Though this is unconventional, especially in a memoir, I feel strongly about incorporating these other voices, particularly of my offspring. Their existence represents my ultimate defiance of Hitler's goal: the extermination of the Jewish people.

Thank you for embarking on this journey with me.

Acknowledgments

I acknowledge Judy Katz's patience in helping me put this book together. It was no easy task to cull through tapes, interviews, and drafts and organize a narrative spanning decades. Thank you, Judy, for your understanding of a difficult chapter in our history. To Mindy Werner: I appreciate your transparency, guidance, and acute understanding of the editing process, which ultimately led me to my publisher. Thank you to Sue Berger Ramin and the entire team at Brandeis University Press, as well as to Judith Cohen of the United States Holocaust Memorial Museum. For assistance and support, thank you to John J. DeGioia, president of Georgetown University; Carole Sargent, director of the Office of Scholarly Publications at Georgetown; and Mel Berger at William Morris Endeavor.

I am grateful to Eleanor Matorin, who, along with many others, welcomed my immigrant family to Gardner, Massachusetts, and became a dear friend to my mother and our entire family. I also recognize two old friends and classmates from Gardner: Levy Garbose and Avi Kamman. The story of my early years would not have been fleshed out as thoroughly without their perspectives and memories.

Levy's uncle acted as sponsor to my father, enabling us to settle in Gardner. Levy witnessed firsthand the adjustments my family, as immigrants, had to make in order to learn a new language and culture. In an interview, he recalled, "I am guessing most Holocaust survivors never said anything to their kids, especially when they came here in the fifties. The smoke was still smoldering in Europe. This was stuff people never dreamed of happening and people didn't talk about it. But everyone gave the whole family great respect. They survived the Holocaust and came to a place where no one even knew what that was."

Avi Kamman's memories of my immigrant family touched me deeply. In an interview, he remarked how my parents were different: "It was like they had been dropped in from another planet. Yet there was something that drew me to them. Hadassah's parents' concerns had a deeper well of meaning behind them. You could tell that they had seen things we hadn't. When I sat with the rabbi and Hadassah's mother, Ella, I could feel that there was something there that was much deeper than the stuff I was involved in, but I didn't know what it was. I realize now I was on the road to looking for G-d, but I didn't yet have the words for G-d."

Michael Davis (Moshi Davidovicz, son of Itzi) represents another important piece of my history; he and his family survived the war thanks in part to the efforts of my mother and her family. How wonderful to have this fellow survivor and relative living in our neighborhood now.

My sincere thanks go to fellow carpooler Lisa Leval. Along with her husband, Gerard, and mine, we have shared many wonderful Shabbat meals together. It was through Lisa that I met Mindy Weisel and her husband, Shelly. When I was having a hard time with my mother, Mindy, whose mother was also a survivor, was just about the only person in my circle who could do more than commiserate; she could completely understand, since she had had similar experiences with her own mother. This was a source of great comfort. Mariella and Michael Trager deserve special thanks for their love and support during the challenging years we lived in Washington. Diane Braunstein, a work colleague and subsequent dear friend, introduced me to DC places beyond Capitol Hill. Marie Carr, another neighbor, was a helpful friend during all of Joe's campaigns and became instrumental in organizing Joe's archives at the Library of Congress. Thank you, Debby Stepelman, for your friendship and editorial support. I also acknowledge Heather Picazio, a staff person in my husband's office, who worked so closely with me throughout the 2000 presidential campaign and after. In addition, I am grateful to Dan Nastu, who has helped me with all my tech needs.

I reserve my greatest acknowledgments for my family. I am grateful to have completed this book in the memory of my parents and in honor of my twelve grandchildren: Nesya, Willie, Maddy, Camilla, Eden, Yitzhak, Yoav, Akiva, Binyamin, Meir, Avraham Shmuel, and Shlomo. I also thank our four children—Matt, Becca, Ethan, and Hani—whose assistance was invaluable. Thanks, too, to my brother, Ary, and sister-in-law, Judy, as well as Joe's sisters, Rietta and Ellen, and their wonderful parents of blessed memory, Marcia and Henry Lieberman. And to my best friend, my Joey: thank you for your ongoing love and support, which made my work on this project that much easier.

HADASSAH

ONE   Momuch

Tell me dear ones what you're learning here
Tell once again and once again

Lyrics from "Ofin Pripichik" ("On the Hearth") | a Yiddish song

I believe that our pasts are not static, something that can be tucked away in a drawer like loose snapshots. The weight of our histories— personal and communal—affects us and propels us. It can also, if we are not careful, haunt us, leaving us hurt, bitter, and unproductive. Ideally, we will react in a way that allows us to preserve its lessons without lingering on the painful ones.

As we age, our understanding of the past grows, or it should. I know that I didn't fully appreciate my mother's history until 2004, shortly after her death. My brother and sister-in-law had previously packed up some of the belongings from my mother's apartment in Riverdale, New York, which my parents had called home since 1978. My father had died in 1993, so now I was going through those last boxes of her belongings.

I went to the apartment with my dear friend Mindy Weisel, a renowned artist born in the Bergen-Belsen concentration camp. Like me, she is the only daughter of Holocaust survivors. Mindy had insisted on helping me with this difficult chore, and I was happy for the company. As we worked, a small leather-bound book slipped to the floor. When I stooped to pick it up, I saw my mother's name embossed on the front cover. Inside were pages and pages in her handwriting. What seemed to be a diary was written in the Czech language. I could make out one or two phrases, but no more, since I never had fluency in the language. When I contacted the US Holocaust Memorial Museum in DC to give them some of my parents' personal items, I asked if they could arrange for a translation of the diary. They gave it to a wonderful woman, Margit Meissner, who was also a survivor and volunteer at the museum who had written her own memoir.

From the first lines of the translation, I was overcome. It began:

Dear Children,

Mama wanted so badly to write for you a diary and each time she tried the memories of her pain destroyed the truth. Maybe one day you will try to say to the world what I could not.

I am writing these few lines in the first hours of the year 1970 with a broken heart because right now I know for sure
I will never write more than this.

Reading these opening lines broke my heart. My mother, Ella Wieder Freilich, was a beautiful woman who radiated confidence and remarkable poise. I called her *Momuch*, a sort of Yiddish/European hybrid word I made up that loosely translates as "my mother." She was equal parts lovable and difficult. Brimming with energy, she possessed a certain kind of Eastern European resourcefulness.

She was also a woman plagued by nightmares. When I was a child, her terrified screams would wake me up in the middle of the night. I would lie in bed fretting about what was wrong with her. I also used to wonder why she was thirty years old when she gave birth to me; it seemed so old for a woman of that time. But was it really so strange for someone whose youth was interrupted by Auschwitz?

From childhood, I had heard snippets of stories of that distant, horrific past. I always listened closely, although she may have thought from my body language that my mind was elsewhere. I was

First page of Hadassah's mother's diary. From the Rabbi
Samuel and Ella Freilich papers at the United States
Holocaust Memorial Museum, Washington, DC.

afraid she might cry too much if she continued talking about her
dark memories—and then she would stop the story and we would
switch to a conversation about a more mundane topic. The stories
were disconnected, seemingly plucked at random from her memory,
and I got the feeling there was much more there, left unspoken. I
remember my mother saying, "Half of me doesn't want to remember
so that I can remain alive."

Her account of the Shoah began when she was twenty-six and
living with her family in the small town of Rachov in the Carpathian
Mountains of Czechoslovakia.

Liberec, November 2, 1945

Diary, I want to write down here a portion of my life from the year 1944.

It was around Passover, when everything was prepared as it usually is to sit down to the festive table when the uniformed Germans with animal facial expressions barged in without even so much as a greeting. . . . My dear mother could not imagine how this could be possible. The German beasts examined our home and did not want to leave. They occupied every room without considering whether there would be room for us to stay there. . . . After a while not one of us had space in our house in which we had lived for forty years. I was the bravest and did not want to show them that I was afraid, so I sat on the chair of one of my siblings in a corner of that formerly beautiful home and read. The reading did not interest me; I just wanted to watch over the things that they called property.

The Germans put phone lines into the walls and set up their headquarters there. They posted notes throughout the small town telling its Jewish inhabitants that they were to report to a local public school, bringing only what they could carry in their hands.

In writing this diary, my mother was able to speak more candidly than she had ever done when I was growing up. The Holocaust had never been a taboo subject in our household. But victims of trauma, especially a trauma of this scale, naturally do not want to relive all the ghastly details. Stories that cannot be uttered aloud, however, can be written. By paying witness through writing, they can communicate an experience that would have remained buried.

At some point after the Germans took over, my mother and her family were taken to Mateszalka, the Hungarian ghetto. The towns-people they had known for years—the neighbors, shopkeepers, and schoolmates—watched as they were taken away, and did nothing. At the camp, my mother remembered a German beating her sister's head. They were then told to line up alphabetically to board trains to Chozov, another town in Czechoslovakia. En route, they could hear some of the local people shouting, "You'll never return." My mother remembered a child's screams for food on the four-day train ride. Some of the other passengers wanted to throw the youngster off the train. A woman whom my mother befriended and eventually settled in New Jersey beseeched them, "Let her be; she is a beautiful young woman."

Then they were taken to Auschwitz:

Through the barred windows we see lots of men and women in striped uniforms. We hear a tremendous roar like if motors were running. We see trucks on which people are stacked and carried. Our senses were not prepared to understand and to take in what we saw and what was happening. Each one of us was terribly weak. When we look out the other barred window we see huge flames. It seems very strange but the optimists among us state that there must be a big fire or they are burning the rags that people brought or somebody said the trash. That fire however was not natural. I compare the fire with a huge storm and lightning that shakes you but is over right away. But there it was night and day. The stench was horrible, and we did not know what it was. We saw all that at night but we did not know what it was. Fear and awe enveloped each one of us. Everybody, even those who did not believe in G-d, started to pray a prayer and promised, if G-d spared them, they would be the best on earth. My dear mother drew us to her with these words: "Come my little children, at least I will have you close to me, press close to me, my child. . . ."

"I had such a hard time to raise you and I was so afraid for you, of G-d." The words got stuck in her throat and she could no longer speak. I could not calm my only mother down, I felt the end was near, I thought what kind of feeling is it when one is not breathing and another parting in the railroad car was not possible. It demolished me so completely that I tried to go to sleep. I was successful.

When I woke up, it was daylight, they open the door a bit with the order that we may not get out of the car. The eyes see the immense length of the train and the width of the railroad station. On the other platform we saw open cars with immense mounds of belongings on the ground that one cannot imagine. The hungry people in my train didn't dare say a word because everywhere it was full of SS. But there were people walking around in striped shirts, sometimes they threw bread into our car and when there was no SS in sight they said to turn the children over to the old ones and to the young, make yourself older [meaning, make yourself look older so you will be selected for work duty and therefore stay alive]. Not all of us understood what that meant so some did not take this very seriously.

My mother told me that when her family came to Auschwitz, some of the Jews who worked at the trains said to them in Yiddish, "You are fools to have come here."

In addition, that first impression of Oswiecim was so perfidious that one could never believe what awaits one. Lots of people, clean barracks, etc. etc. Then came the moment when we had to leave the railroad car. I don't know exactly what time it was, maybe 10 in the morning, the whole family gathered together, so that we should not lose each other. We walk a few hundred steps, in front of the gate. I do not notice a burly, fat SS man who pushes me to the right and I can't see where my family was. I shout at him: "I want to stay with mummy." He didn't even react but he pushed me and I got sick and didn't know where I was. When I repeat I want to stay with mummy, he answered: "You will see her this evening." I believed him and trundled after the other women who were on the same side as I. We go on an endlessly long road, I see blocks, wire, channels, sand and earth. The blocks were so extensive that the human eye could not see to the end. We finally got into a huge space that they called *Raum* [room].

We were still properly dressed when we entered this space; they told us to get undressed, all naked. We could not understand that. We see men, so how is that possible, but they started to be strict with us. They yelled so there was nothing we could do. We stand there naked. If there had been only a few of us, it would have been terrible but because we were several thousand, one got lost in the crowd. I stood in a row with a friend and a man in a striped jacket who was smoking. My friend would have been happy to have a cigarette, she made a gesture to that effect and the man offered her and me a cigarette. We have a good smoke. I feel like asking him why they brought us here and I completely forget that I am naked. That prisoner in the striped jacket could not tell us much because we had to walk on to get our heads shaved. G-d, I think, what good would my hair be to them? But I don't have much time; I already want to have it behind me. My hair was cut and I saw the blond locks on the floor, they shone like gold.

We continue, we bathe and again inspection to see if we don't have anything on us, some jewel or similar. We get a grey long dress, one shirt, a pair of pants, that's all they gave us. We didn't have any of the other things that a woman needs but 99% we didn't need; we didn't have a towel or any other vital items. We continue walking, a catastrophic spectacle when we saw each other. Powerful rainfall washed us as we continued walking. They still did not give us anything to eat although for the whole trip we had nothing. We arrived in an office, rather a hall where we had to state our name, year of birth and place of origin.

Finally, we get into a block number 14A. They counted us and we were more than 1400 persons. Can anybody imagine what kind of noise and yelling there was. The first day we didn't know yet about the disciplinarian. But it didn't even take twelve hours the next day, at three in the morning they start yelling, "Aufsstehen [get up], gehen Kafee holen [go get coffee]," the people didn't know that that means that they had to get up but they soon found out. They were so trained to notice the person who was moving slowly, who had said to herself, "I still have a few minutes." She would be the first one prodded into getting up. That is how it went day and night. The weather in Oswiecim was different from that in central Europe. When it started to rain, such high water and mud was standing on the courtyard or rather the Appellplatz that it came up to your knees. But if the sun shone, it was worse than in the Sahara.

Every one of us had blue lips because one did not get enough water. There were *Waschraume*, washrooms, but there wasn't enough time for all of us to get there because at 9 o'clock they tried to make order even if people were dying of thirst and hunger. If somebody fainted, it was very hard to get her a few drops of water. As I write I myself cannot believe that it was true. The camp was divided into groups A, B, C. When you looked from one camp into the other, you had the impression of seeing another world. One always saw so many people there, only an electrified barbed wire separated us and of course the extent, the human eye could see that far but was not able to recognize anybody.

I always said to myself that my family and my relatives are most likely behind that barbed wire. Although daily we heard the news that our relatives were burned to death we did not believe it. We always believed that they live somewhere in another block because we saw some old person, or a sick person, etc. And so our eyes deceived us.

Sadly, that was all Mother wrote. I wish that she had left us much more. And yet, I understand. The times she describes were the worst, and she could only write so much. Unbelievably, she had never once mentioned having written this diary, and it was only by chance that we found it. When I finally read the translation, I was overcome with emotion. What I would give for even one more hour with my mother—one hour to tell her how much I loved her. And yet, even with its discovery, there are still so many unanswered questions. What was my mother doing in Liberec, in what is now the Czech Republic, on November 2, 1945—the date and place listed in the diary? Perhaps she was in a sanatorium there, recovering from the war. I recall her mentioning that she'd spent time in a facility, and there was an old villa in the town used for that purpose. If this is the case, then it makes sense that she would begin keeping a diary while she was regaining her strength. And if she did start writing her diary there, it means she carried it with her when she came to America with her husband and infant daughter and kept it hidden for decades. I wish I knew what caused her to start writing again in 1970, after twenty-five years had passed.

It's also curious that she wrote the diary in Czech, a more formal language than the Hungarian she relied on when writing letters. Maybe she wrote in Czech because more people at the sanatorium used that language, and she'd gotten accustomed to it. The language in the diary is much more formal than her actual speech, although that could be a function of the translation. Also, I never asked my mother why she didn't have a number tattooed on her arm, like the others who survived the camps. I've always wondered about this but could never bring myself to question her. I suppose there are limits to what you want to know.

We donated my mother's diary to the United States Holocaust Memorial Museum in Washington, DC.

The Nazi soldiers never talked to any Jews. They thought they were disgusting. My grandmother couldn't remember seeing any Nazi talk to anyone but Nazis, except for one time. A Nazi guard once asked her if she could speak German. She said yes. Then he asked her to tell him one wish that she had. She thought, "I couldn't wish for my family to be alive, because I knew they were already dead." So she wished she could sleep one night, after nine months of not sleeping, without having to be worried for her life. . . . She told me that G-d was with her and whispered in her ear what to say.

HANI LIEBERMAN | daughter

I think Momuch wanted me to find her diary and knew I would do what I could to share her story. When the *New York Times* interviewed her during the run-up to the 2000 election, all she would say about her wartime experience was, "We came from hell." It is a strange feeling when the pain of the past comes into contact with gratitude in the present. I suppose this is what people mean when they speak of the healing process.

My mother was one of the fortunate ones: she lived. Yet like all other survivors, she carried the weight of what she had experienced for the rest of her life. It is part of me too, embedded in my DNA. Now it is my turn—and, yes, also my children's and my children's children, to carry this weight, as well as the awareness of the hope that accompanied it. In an essay written in 1998, when she was just sixteen, my niece, Sarah, my brother Ary's daughter, completed my mother's wartime story, based on interviews with her:

My grandmother, Ella, was born in Rachov, Czechoslovakia, in 1918. She and her husband, Samuel Freilich, were the first in both of their families to settle in America, in 1949. They came to America because they lost most of their families in the war, in concentration camps. They came with their newborn daughter, Hadassah Esther, who was about 9 months old. My grandfather, Samuel, was born in Torun, Czechoslovakia, in 1902.

From Rachov, Ella and her family were taken by train to a ghetto, and then to Auschwitz, the murder place as she called it. During this time Nazi soldiers took over her house. She was in her twenties, and still living with her mother and one of her sisters. The other one lived in a house behind theirs, and her brother lived nearby as well. Her father had died because of asthma a few years earlier. While they were in the ghetto, she heard from a neighbor that one of her cousins was shot and thrown into a river in Rachov, called the Dnieper River. The people thrown in there were to be eaten by animals.

At Auschwitz there were hundreds of people. As she came closer to the front of the line of people, she could tell what was happening. The soldiers were sending some people one way, to be killed, and other people another way to suffer, but not die. It was her family's turn. They walked up to the soldier, holding hands in a chain, clearly showing that they didn't want to be separated, but the soldier did it anyway. He sent my grandmother's entire family one way, to be killed, and her the other way. As she walked in the opposite way of the rest of her family, all of them crying, her sister, Rozi, snuck under the mass of the people and reached Ella. She didn't get caught, and the two of them were sent to get their hair shaved off. My grandmother took great pride in her hair, and turned around to refuse. As she turned around, she saw her other sister, Suri, being whipped on the head with a leather strap, by a woman Nazi, for refusing to walk to a gas chamber. Then she saw her grandmother whipped because she refused to go to the bathroom. She never saw her family ever again. She decided not to put up a fight.

At night all the people on her side had to march in Auschwitz, and sleep during the day. She couldn't sleep during the day. She couldn't adjust to sleeping in daylight, and staying up at night. Besides being tired all the time, they were all starving. They were given one piece of bread, and one glass of water a day.

Then they were all taken to Guistlingen [near Stuttgart, to the Wehrmacht Fabrik factory, where they worked as slave laborers] and all the people had to take clothes off the dead people laying on the ground. There the Jews were brought to a factory and had to help build guns that were going to be used to kill more Jews.

She left that town, and was brought to another town. This was where the soldiers began killing women. She was praying that she wouldn't be called. One of the soldiers gave her an extra piece of bread. She was so excited that she wrote him a letter of thank you. Someone found the letter, and a woman Nazi came over to her, and asked her who gave her the bread. She figured that if she told her who it was she would die, and so would the soldier, and if she didn't tell, she would also die. She told me that G-d was with her, and whispered in her ear what to say. She said, "I found the bread in a barrel, and I wanted to thank whoever put it there." The woman let her go.

She saw chaos everywhere, when she marched out of that town and left for Alac-Dachau. She marched through the forest, stepping on all the dead bodies laying in their paths. She wanted to run. She knew she couldn't and shouldn't, but she wanted to. When she got to the next town, the Nazi soldiers let them go. They were free. Everyone ran as fast as they could, before they could change their minds. As she and her sister Rozi ran they saw black smoke coming from the burning chambers, and heard shrieks of terror in the camps.

As my grandmother later told me, they wound up back in

their hometown. There was a man there, a druggist, who had known Ella. He also knew Rabbi Samuel Freilich. He was the man who encouraged my grandparents to meet. Ella wouldn't go meet him, she was nervous, so she sent Rozi to meet him first. Rozi went to Prague to meet him, and came back with good news. She liked him a lot, and thought that her sister Ella would like him too. They met, and in 1947 they got married in Prague. In 1948 they had their first child, Hadassah.

As I said at her funeral, Mother loved nature and was herself a force of nature: genuine, nurturing, beautiful, full of surprises. Now she is gone, but the memories she leaves with us and the lessons she taught are now part of our life force. They are her legacy to us—our responsibility to keep alive. In truth this was one of my motivations for writing this book. I wanted to fix in print what my mother could not, and describe her strength.

TWO

Daddy

It is incumbent upon every Jew to remember the Shoah.
For if not we, then who? If we fail to remind the world, who will?
And who should say the mourner's Kaddish, if not we?

From *The Coldest Winter: The Holocaust Memoirs*
of Rabbi Samuel Freilich, Hadassah's father

As children, we sometimes try to imagine our parents at younger ages, before they even knew that we would exist. Photographs give us a glimpse of those earlier times, and family members might share their jokes to flesh out imaginative reflections of their parents. What was she like as a child? Did he play in that park?

What a contrast to try and imagine a past when nearly everything was marked for destruction. Few if any relatives remain, although occasionally a former neighbor is discovered, maybe living in another country or a distant city. Miraculously, some photographs and memoir pieces appear, providing a little with which to piece the history together. Later, someone might ask the elderly survivor to record an oral history, but one wonders, *Who will want to listen?* Now it is too late. My parents are gone, and the number of Holocaust survivors still with us is dwindling.

My father used to say that it would take a thousand years for people to understand the Holocaust. It is in fact difficult to absorb the overwhelming experience of it. Here is my daddy's story.

One of six children, he was born on April 16, 1903, in Torun, Hungary, near the Carpathian Mountains. The boys—my father and his three brothers, Menachem, Hersch, and Moshe—received a traditional Jewish education from the age of three. A few years later, my father spent weeknights sleeping on the stove at his uncle's place, since this was close to the yeshiva he was then attending. He would come home to his parents for the weekend.

A very small percentage of the population in the area was Jewish. Hasidic rabbis, especially the Satmar Rebbe, Joel Teitelbaum, were in charge of religious matters. (Founded in 1905 by Rabbi Teitelbaum in Szatmarnemeti, Hungary, the Satmars are a Hasidic group.) Jews and Gentiles lived side by side in relative piece, eking out a living by working as day laborers in the lumber and agriculture industries. After World War I, when Hungary lost the region to Czechoslovakia, this remote town was brought into the modern era.

My father's connection to the outside world was through his brother Menachem, whose horizons had expanded during his sojourns to Switzerland. (Their brother Hersch had immigrated to the United States in 1909.) My grandmother, hypersensitive to the neighbors' criticism, would stuff photos of Menachem —who wore no head covering and did not have a beard—into a dresser drawer. He also introduced my father to such ideologies as Zionism, which Menachem was exposed to in Zurich while working as a teacher, and of which the Satmar Rebbe disapproved. In time, Menachem relocated to Brno (Brunn, as it was known in German) and headed its chapter of the Jewish Social Democratic Labor Party, known as Poale Zion.

In the 1920s, the state-appointed administrators of the Jewish community in Czechoslovakia wanted to enlist young men to work as teachers and rabbis. Suitable candidates from Torun would be given a secular education along with funds to cover their living expenses. As much as my father wanted to go, his parents were equally passionate that he continue with his traditional religious education.

But my father had made up his mind. He was one of the eleven students chosen, and off he went to Prague. His parents were not happy about this and let him know that he should not expect any assistance from them.

For three years, the young men studied mathematics, languages, and philosophy. They soon cut off their sidelocks and no longer wore the typical Hasidic attire, but their singsong delivery in class, uttered while rocking from side to side, stayed the same. Their instructors found it entertaining.

All eleven students successfully completed their course work and progressed to universities. My father decided to study law at Charles University in Prague, one of the continent's most enlightened academic institutions. Once there, he gravitated to the Jewish student organization, whose members were all Zionists. My father now had a foot in several disparate cultures, a situation he was especially conscious of when he visited his parents.

In 1934, when he completed his law studies, he was appointed as rabbi to the Jewish community of Bohemia-Moravia with a liberal congregation in Leitomischl (Litomysl). With the 1938 annexation of Austria, Germany's sights were now set on Czechoslovakia. The German invasion would completely alter the course of my father's life and those of all other European Jews. His congregation folded, and then he moved to Brno to join Menachem and his family.

Hersch requested an American visa for my father, but by the time it arrived, it was useless because the Roosevelt administration had closed the door to Eastern European immigrants. My father also sought the assistance of American congregations—securing a job would enable him to get a US visa—but no help was forthcoming. Since Hungary annexed the Transcarpathian region of Czechoslovakia, he claimed Hungarian citizenship, which meant he did not need to wear the Jewish star as required of his Czech friends. Menachem obtained a visa to Palestine and immigrated with his wife and children.

In 1940, my father also received a Palestine visa. When he picked it up at the Gestapo office, he was asked where he was heading en route to the Holy Land. When my father said, "Budapest," the official warned him, "We will follow; be sure to go farther."

In Budapest, my father found that Jewish life seemed to have returned to normal, so he didn't feel the need to rush to Palestine. After spending the winter of 1940 there, he went to visit friends and family in Munkacz. There, he was conscripted into a Hungarian forced labor camp. After several weeks, he was allowed to return home, but that summer he was enlisted to build fortifications on the Yugoslav border. By the time he was released, his travel papers had become invalid. My father accepted a job teaching Hebrew in Munkacz, only to be conscripted yet again the following autumn. Of the roughly sixty thousand Hungarian Jews who were pressed into service, only fifteen thousand would survive the forced march. Hungarian gendarmes loaded the Jewish conscripts on a train heading east, finally reaching Minsk in January 1943. Hungarian military police required them to strip, beat them, and forced them to perform calisthenics before making them march toward the front. They arrived at Ostrogozhsk on the Don River, where they stayed in abandoned Russian huts, but within a few hours, they had to resume their march to escape advancing Russian troops.

My father's brigade began marching west through deep snow. The Jews were not issued rations, but some Belorussian peasants shared their food. During the march, a truck ran over my father's foot. At first the Hungarian captain refused to allow him to ride in a military vehicle, but he eventually relented after my father gently warned that the man would need to account to G-d for his actions. My father became separated from his original unit but continued west, joining up with others until he eventually arrived in Ukraine. By spring 1943, the snow began to melt, but by then, many of the Jews, including my father, had contracted typhus. The retreat was halted on the outskirts of Lvov, and the Hungarians decided to quarantine the Jewish typhus victims in a former Russian cooperative, Doroschitz. My father called it "the Hungarian Auschwitz." The makeshift hospital had neither beds nor medicine; thousands of Jews died there and were buried in an unmarked grave. When my father left Doroschitz, he weighed seventy pounds, was blind in one eye, and was debilitated by rheumatism, but he was alive.

Eventually the Hungarian government recalled what was left of the Jewish battalions and sent them back by passenger train to Budapest to recuperate. The Jewish conscripts couldn't believe that they were now treated like the Gentile soldiers, given warm food, beds, and medical care. At the Hungarian border, my father wept when he heard a military band playing "Ave Maria," which would never have previously provoked such a response. It was not lost on him that exactly one year prior, at this train station, he had begun his death march to the Russian front.

After his release, my father briefly worked in the Hungarian city of Chust as a Hebrew school principal, though he was officially on leave from his work brigade. However, he soon had to rejoin his brigade and was dispatched to the Austrian border to build anti-tank traps and bunkers. In December 1944, Russian troops were deep in Hungary, and his brigade was forced to march to the Schachendorf labor camp in Austria. The workers again built fortifications and received barely any food. A friend from Munkacz served as camp leader and appointed my father to be his secretary. My father assigned hospital passes to those who were sick. That changed when he learned that instead of taking the infirm Jews to a hospital, a German soldier removed them from the camp and shot them. My father then established a work rotation to keep the weakest men away from the "hospital" but also allowed them to rest. In March 1945, the Germans evacuated Schachendorf, and the prisoners were sent on a death march to Auschwitz. My father managed to escape with twenty other men by pretending they were Hungarian farmers fleeing the Russians.

Then came liberation, but it was not the joyous event one might expect. Here is how my father recalls it in his memoir:

> We experienced no catharsis. . . . We did not drink or dance or laugh. It had been ten years since Hitler had said he would make the Jews forget how to laugh, and truly we had forgotten how. Fear had dominated our lives for so long that we still found it beyond belief that we had outlasted Hitler's 'Thousand-Year Reich.'"

My father may have been free, but he wasn't sure where to go. His congregation in Leitomischl had perished, along with his students in Chust and his family in Torun. My father wrote:

> The Jews of Czechoslovakia, their Zionist organizations, political parties, cultural organizations and Hebrew schools all had been pulled up by the roots without protest by the good Czechs with whom we had lived for so many generations. They knew what the Germans were doing to the Jews, yet the vast majority of them stood by silently, waiting to inherit our wealth. I could not bear the thought of going home and seeing gentiles standing in the threshold of Jewish homes, synagogues and schools.

In 1945, he decided to travel to Budapest, where the greatest number of Jewish survivors had gathered. In consultation with the rabbinic seminary, which had continued to operate during the war, he helped establish schools for Jewish war orphans in Budapest, Debrecin, and Sighet, funded by the Joint Distribution Committee. My father also became involved in politics.

In time, he moved to Prague and met my mother. They married in Prague's Altneuschul (the Old New Synagogue) in February 1947. I was born the following March. The next year the Soviet Union took over. My parents had survived the Nazis by the grace of G-d and were not going to risk that gift by living under another oppressive regime. We left Prague and immigrated to the United States.

"Where was G-d?" I remember my father asking. "Where was G-d?" and he, a rabbi, deeply believed in Him. How could you ever believe again? "Faith was the cornerstone of our existence," he wrote in his memoirs. "It was inconceivable to us that a merciful father could ignore the pitiful pleas of his children. When we were delivered to the Nazis and the redemption did not occur, we fell into despair; life lost meaning. . . . We became an orphan people without a heavenly father."

Even in the face of calamity my father always believed there was some purpose to everything in life. He wasn't obsessed with determining *why* he had survived when so many hadn't. He wasn't particularly concerned with ruminating over the part that luck, chance, or fate might have played. Rather, the questions he asked were: Since I survived, what kind of life am I going to lead? What responsibilities do I have? How can I make sure I did not survive in vain?

For my father, the answer was to move forward. He was too modest about the role he played during and after the war, but he was a genuine hero, helping to stop the deportation from Czechoslovakia of two thousand Carpathian Jewish refugees. My father accepted the horrors of the past. He wanted us to accept our lives and keep going, no matter how difficult the path might be. The things that truly mattered to him were faith, family, service, and educating the next generation about what those things really mean. My brother, Ary, and I were taught to see ourselves as important and to believe that anything was possible in our lives if we worked hard for it, consistently and without self-doubt.

When I learned that my grandfather had passed away, a strange mixture of joy and sadness was thrust upon me. After all, this day of Simchat Torah, which had always marked a time of happiness, excitement, and the date of my grandfather's birth, now marked the beginning of a new chapter in all of our lives and the day of my grandfather's death. Our tradition tells us that it is a sign of special divine attention when one is born and dies on the same day—that an element of *shlemut* (completeness) is present.

For me, Zeydee was a multidimensional character. When I was very young, I recall returning home with him several times a week from nursery school, and on the journey home we would sing "Adon Olam" together. I can't even remember what the context was for this, but it was one of those special moments that are difficult to forget.

As I grew older, I began to appreciate how Zeydee wanted great things from his grandchildren. He had little tolerance for anything that seemed to him a waste of time. Many times when I was watching a cartoon, he would simply enter the room, pick up the remote control, and change the channel. As a five-year-old, this was a difficult concept to deal with, but it was indicative of Zeydee's firm beliefs as to what values in life are important.

A side of Zeydee that I appreciated more as I matured was his place in history. Even before he recorded his memoirs, I thought of him as a fierce Zionist, and I was fascinated by his struggle with G-d in the aftermath of the war. Zeydee put great stock in the Jewish people, and his survival through their modern catastrophe made this side of him that much more powerful.

An excerpt from Rabbi Ethan Tucker's eulogy for his grandfather

THREE My Immigrant Identity

You shall not oppress a stranger,
for you know the feelings of a stranger, having yourselves
been strangers in the land of Egypt.

EXODUS 23:9

If I had to summarize the essence of the American immigrant experience in a single word, I would choose *promise*. I've met thousands of my fellow immigrants, and promise runs through us like current through copper wire. The word itself, *promise*, means both a vow that something will happen and the potential for achievement. These are the assurances that bolster the courage of those who leave their country and set out in search of a better life. It is also a good descriptor for the American shores on which they land. Every immigrant believes that the opportunity to advance socially, economically, and personally in this country is more than a possibility; it has the certainty of a promise.

I'm not suggesting that immigrants view the United States as a utopia where all of their problems magically disappear. Immigrating to a new country has never been easy. It can be an arduous, sometimes terrifying, and often disorienting experience. Immigrants find themselves uprooted from all that is familiar, in a place where the food seems strange, the language indecipherable, the culture endlessly confusing. The dislocation that comes from living far from extended family and facing the difficulty of finding work can be daunting. Even minor differences can make them stand out in a way that has them questioning where they belong. It is a willing sacrifice, yes, but a sacrifice nonetheless.

As I write, these are especially anxious times for immigrants. Though xenophobia has always existed, it seems to have increased of late. For sure, we need rules about who can enter our country, and we have to watch our borders, but I believe that if we view immigrants with respect, they will view themselves with respect, and that is crucial to moving forward together. The vast majority of new arrivals will contribute to our country, cherishing our best traditions of democracy and equality and elevating us to new heights with their accomplishments. As an immigrant myself, I feel it is my duty to extend the same generous welcome to new immigrants that my family felt when we came here. I hope we return to the mind-set that America is a place that welcomes immigrants, not a distrustful nation that regards newcomers with resentment.

Let's not forget that America has *always* been a nation of immigrants. The greatness of our country traditionally has been our acceptance of people from so many different backgrounds, religions, and cultures. Even in our melting pot society, there has been a tolerance of one another and an understanding of the need for polite discourse. Hitler's Germany showed how quickly ugly speech can infect a culture and lead to disastrous consequences. Until recently, most people in this country have never feared such a scenario. This seems to be changing, and it's a dangerous turn of events. As the oft-quoted philosopher George Santayana said, "Those who cannot remember the past are condemned to repeat it." Our democracy starts with our leadership. Our elected officials, corporate and civic leaders, teachers and parents must reinforce the message that our country embraces and supports immigrants. The offensive, incendiary language that some of our leaders are using must stop; they need to set the example. Only through their mindful actions will our children get the message and treat immigrants with the respect they deserve. We must do this for the future of the nation, so that we nurture a generation of young people we can be proud of and who will light the way for subsequent generations.

My own story begins in Prague, where I was born in 1948. My given name is Esther, after my maternal grandmother who was killed by the Nazis. When my father went to register my birth certificate with the Czech authorities, he was told that the name sounded "too German." My father agreed to a change, and I was named Hadassah. He didn't change my name completely, just officially, since *Hadassah* is Hebrew for Esther, as in the biblical Queen Esther.

World War II had been over for only about three years, and its impact still dominated nearly every sphere of public life. Some people were moving to Israel, but my mother didn't want to go because of the war there. Through HIAS (Hebrew Immigrant Aid Society), our small family of three immigrated to the United States, traveling by ship as most immigrants did. Apparently on the crossing, the captain twirled me around the dance floor while some fellow passengers suffered from seasickness. My mother often spoke about how thrilling it was to enter New York Harbor under the watchful eye of Lady Liberty.

We wound up in Brooklyn, New York, where my father worked odd jobs to earn enough money to get us started. When they thought my parents weren't listening, our Jewish neighbors referred to us as "greenhorns," a derogatory term for inexperienced or naive individuals, newcomers to a country who are unacquainted with local manners and customs. My mother never forgot how that expression stung.

As my father told me subsequently, at that time a lot of Orthodox rabbis from Europe were offered positions in Conservative synagogues in America, especially in New England. Apparently the Conservative movement had budgets to assist these rabbinic refugees. My father contacted rabbinical figures and eventually secured sponsorship from a colleague living in the small town of Gardner, Massachusetts, a welcoming New England city of about twenty thousand people. A classic New England industrial town in north-central Massachusetts, not too far from the New Hampshire border, it was a center for furniture making—beds, cribs, and couches—symbolized by the giant chair located on the outskirts of town. For us, it might as well have been another planet. I was only two years old then, but I recall some events vividly. My first memory of Gardner is of being registered as an immigrant. I don't know why we had to sign up there in addition to going through customs and immigration at Ellis Island. At that time, a local order of Catholic nuns was in charge of this task. For some reason, my father told the nun who was examining my forms that he had originally wanted to name me Esther but had been discouraged from doing so by the Czech authorities. He wondered if he might change it back now from Hadassah to give me a more "American-sounding" name. The nun looked at my birth certificate and said, "Rabbi, don't change her name. It is unique. Don't change it to Esther: Hadassah is a beautiful name."

In those few sentences, she articulated the vast difference between where we had come from and where we had landed. This nun was telling us that my name, an explicitly *Jewish* name, was not only acceptable but *beautiful* and, further, that it was beautiful precisely because it was distinctive. To tell an immigrant father that his young daughter's Hebrew name is worthy and that it will remind people of beauty every time they utter it is an incredible act of inclusivity and kindness.

We first lived in a small apartment, but my father, as the new rabbi, was soon given a modest house on Reservoir Road, where my parents did their best to adjust to this new way of life. In my younger years, my mother's vegetable garden fed us with its bounty. As she worked the earth, she would recall the beautiful pears her mother grew in her childhood backyard a lifetime ago. The European custom of taking long walks continued with our daily—and mandatory—strolls around the reservoir at the top of our street, regardless of the weather. My brother and I scampered around while my parents conversed.

Sunday was family day. In the summer we'd pick blueberries and blackberries and have picnics. There was sledding, ice skating, and watching the ice fishermen and their huskies in the cold months. As we got older, my brother and I helped our father shovel snow, even when it piled up so high that we couldn't open the back door to our house. As we worked, the frost blasted our faces. When we came inside, the kitchen windows would be steamy from the vegetable soup my mother had made.

Only about thirty Jewish families lived in Gardner then. Most owned businesses: a pharmacy, a clothing store, a junkyard. What separated those families from the ones we had known back in Europe was that their main goal in life was upward social and financial mobility, not religious piety or identity. They considered themselves to be Americans first and Jews second, which placed another barrier between my family and everyone else. An old school pal of mine remarked that my family was an odd entry into that small New England town, the only observant household there. Every week in our house, the challah was made from scratch and the smell of chicken soup permeated the air. The Shabbat table was always set with a white cloth, and *tzibele mit ei*—chopped hard-boiled eggs and onions—was a regular meal for Shabbat lunch. No one ever sat in my father's seat, and *balabustah* (a good homemaker) was the highest compliment my mother could give or be given. On Saturday afternoons after lunch and a discussion of the *parsha*, the Torah portion for that week, and *Pirkei Avot*, a compilation of rabbinical teachings on ethics, all four of us would sit on the oversized porch swing and relax together.

While some of the other Jewish families kept kosher in the home, we were the only ones we knew of who kept kosher "in and out," meaning at home and in restaurants. The closest kosher butcher was in Worcester, about a fifty-minute drive south. I'd accompany my parents on these outings. Once there, we'd load up on groceries at what we called "the kosher store," one of the kosher bakeries and delis on Water Street, the center of Jewish Worcester's commercial life. On the way home, we'd munch on rye bread and cold cuts—a real treat.

My father had been instructed to apply a Conservative rather than an Orthodox interpretation of Judaism for his congregation. All of the Jewish families attended services on the holidays, but far fewer came to worship on a regular basis, though there was always a *minyan*, the gathering of ten men needed in order to say certain prayers. Those who drove to the synagogue on Shabbat parked a block away and walked to the building out of respect for my father, who as an observant Jew didn't drive on the Sabbath. My father's sermons were always well received, since he had a deep well of Judaic knowledge, and his life lessons and practical advice won him an avid following—not only among the Jewish families but throughout the town.

I don't recall any anti-Semitism in Gardner, overt or more subtle. We always felt that we were a part of the community and were never shunned because of my parents' accents, our background, or our religious practice. In fact, as just one measure of how welcoming the town was, when I was in high school, the administration switched the night of the prom so it wouldn't conflict with the Sabbath and I could go.

My parents were the town's only Holocaust survivors. What significance this had overall, I am not entirely sure. Many people in America were not yet familiar with the gruesome details of the war; that would come later. I do know that my parents retained a certain European exoticness. That is how we probably appeared to many people, though we were just trying to be Americans.

My parents were a handsome couple. My father, clean shaven, was of moderate height with a kindly mien. His wireless glasses gave him an Old World, academic air. People were at least familiar with the concept of an Orthodox rabbi, but my mother was a different creature altogether. She had a charming accent and was a gorgeous woman who couldn't have been more different from the typical housewife of that place and era. She was in her mid-thirties, seventeen years younger than my father, and no matter how little money we had, she always found a way to dress with a certain glamorous flair. She favored heels, and her hair was always done up with what looked to me like sticks used to keep everything in place. In truth, had their circumstances been different, my parents might not have ended up together. But my father appreciated her charm and beauty, and she appreciated his wisdom and erudition.

Beneath the charm, my mother was strong-willed, and like many mothers and daughters, we had our clashes. Maybe some of this was because of her difficult history. My friend Mindy Weisel and I have discussed this often, since we are both only daughters of survivors. As Mindy puts it, "We both had to forgive our mothers for their weaknesses and tragedies. When you have damaged mothers, there's a lot you're not allowed to be angry at them about. You forgive them for what they were not able to give you. It's not that they didn't want to; it's just that they weren't able."

In addition, my mother and I clashed because she was a strong woman raising a strong daughter who was encouraged to have her own opinions and use her voice. My mother too wasn't afraid to express her opinion about anything. If she didn't like how my hair or dress looked, she told me. If she thought I was overly verbal, she would say, "No man likes a woman who talks so much." She was impatient and not the quiet, let-the-kids-figure-it-out kind of parent. Always, though, I adored and respected her. I understood and accepted that she was from another time and place. I miss her.

Although most of my mother's family had perished, her sister,

Rozi, lived in Brooklyn, where she and her husband ran a laundry. Maybe because they had no children of their own, my aunt doted on me. I spent chunks of time there in the summer, helping out in the business. Aside from this connection to her past, my mother never sought out other Holocaust survivors and never pushed me to do so.

When I was in high school, I learned of a gathering of survivors taking place in Worcester and decided to go. I was surprised at how few people attended the event and ended up writing an editorial for a local paper lamenting this fact. In later years, I was surprised to discover that many such groups existed, offering survivors and their families the opportunity to share their commonality of experience. It just wasn't something that was part of my parents' lives.

Momuch's experiences imbued her with a composure that made people take notice when she entered a room and listen to her when she spoke. It was impossible to ignore her presence; you had to *contend* with it. Certainly anyone on the street had to contend with her when she drove us to school because she was a notoriously reckless driver. People never got upset—partially, I think, because they weren't entirely sure what to make of her: a beautiful rabbi's wife who barely spoke English, zigzagging down the road of this little New England town, waving at her bemused neighbors. That image makes me smile to this day.

From an early age, I understood that my parents saw my brother and me as proof and purpose of their survival. That was the gift— and the responsibility—they gave to us. It was not a theoretical or inspirational ideal but a true obligation, and heaven help us if we failed to do well in school and didn't make something of ourselves! What other choice was there? One of my father's favorite Hebrew sayings, *eyn brayrah*, roughly translates as "no choice." It's one of those phrases that doesn't have an exact equivalent in English. But in the American immigrant experience, it had ample opportunity to make sense.

Ary and I had to make sure our actions were true to ourselves, but also that they did justice to those who had been killed. Many of those who died never had the chance to have children, so in a way we had to act as *their* children. We had to redeem the lives they never got to lead. The Holocaust charged us—the survivors, their children, and their children's children—with a quest for meaning. It was our responsibility, as the lucky ones, to live purpose-driven lives in honor of all those who had died. Every breath we took was a refutation of evil and an opportunity to leave our mark on the world. We weren't guilt-tripped into feeling this way; it was just how it was. My parents were very matter-of-fact in their parenting. They didn't encourage us to figure out how we should act in a given situation: they simply *told* us what to do and expected that we would do it. It's a completely different approach, so unlike much of today's child-centered parenting.

From an early age, I got the message. On my first day of kindergarten, my mother braided my hair as usual and put little bows on the sides. I was never allowed to go anywhere with my hair loose; it always had to be braided, or at least in a tight ponytail. She walked me to school, which wasn't too far from our home. There were all these kids wearing different kinds of clothing, and most of the girls wore pants. I wasn't allowed to wear them, even in winter. I held on to the lunchbox my mother had packed earlier and listened to the kids speak a language I could not understand. At that point, I spoke only Yiddish, with the exception of a few basic English phrases, like, "Thank you," "Hello," and "Goodbye." There I was in this strange environment, listening and watching, straining to understand. I decided that I would just follow the other kids and try to do what they did.

After our lessons, the teacher held a basket above our heads and asked us to each raise a hand and pull something out of it. You could choose a wonderful surprise—a little hard candy or a toy car. This was an almost daily occurrence, and for me it came to symbolize abundance and everything this new world held for me: a basketful of treats would be yours if you were good and worked hard. On that very first day of school, I committed to becoming totally American—and, over time, to becoming not only American but an *exceptional* American who would make my parents and my country proud.

When I got home, my mother asked me in Yiddish about my first day. I said, "No more Yiddish, Momma, only English." If I was going to be like everyone else, I had to speak everyone else's language.

"Dus es goot," she said. "That is good." From that point on, learning English became a driving force in my life. I didn't only want to learn English; I wanted to learn English like an American or, rather, *as* an American, and by the first grade, I was proficient. As a result, although I grew up in a house where Czech and Yiddish were spoken frequently, I never had an accent. Many of my childhood friends tell me they can't remember me speaking anything but perfectly unaccented English.

My father worked diligently to perfect his English, which was necessary since he had to use the language to give his sermons. Many nights I fell asleep to the sound of his voice on the tape recorder he used to practice this new language. Here he was, an immigrant and survivor in his mid-forties, starting anew in a foreign land, adapting to a new culture, home, and language—his sixth. My mother, with no such imperative or deadline, was never quite able to grasp the language. She knew Czech, Hungarian, Yiddish, German, and Polish but found English to be the most challenging of the bunch. She got upset with herself because she found it nearly impossible to master the spelling. She would go to women's club meetings in town at the urging of her friends and then couldn't understand much of what was being said. It was a difficult process and painful to watch her struggling.

As is the case with many immigrants and their children, the language barrier created a new dynamic between us. She depended on me for matters both large and small. I helped her sign checks, translate simple phrases, and call a doctor's office for an appointment. It gave me a sense of purpose as a young girl and made me even more committed to forge an American identity out of my immigrant one. I would not only become an American; I would help my mother become one as well.

That sense of responsibility has stuck with me. I felt a need to help my parents and take care of them. My brother and I were their "stars in the sky," as they often put it—their reason for going on after the Holocaust. I knew the best way to meet their expectations would be to succeed in life, and to do that I had to succeed in my studies. Since my parents couldn't help me with my homework, it was all on me. I applied myself in school and did well. I also made efforts to become part of the community beyond the synagogue, involving myself in activities like Brownies and Girl Scouts and, later, student life and social organizing. No dating though: I was an Orthodox rabbi's daughter, after all! In my father's view, dating was serious business that you did only to confirm that you were a good match with the person you intended to marry. Above all, we were taught the importance of family and to stick together, no matter what. I have done my best to pass this value along to my children.

I remember when I won the "I Speak for Democracy" contest in high school. Young people from across the state had been invited to submit essays on the topic, and I worked hard on my submission. I'm sure my father edited it; I can't imagine he would have let me apply without his input. On that Memorial Day, I got to ride in a convertible as part of the town parade, sitting next to our Massachusetts congressman, Philip Philbin, and waving an American flag. It was an important moment for my parents, who beamed from the crowd. They were intensely patriotic Americans.

Recently one of my grandsons asked what I did for fun when I was his age. I told him that I didn't think about things like that. I had too much else to focus on and accomplish. For starters, there was my background. While the other kids in Gardner might hear lighthearted stories about their parents' youthful antics, the stories in our house were much heavier—sometimes even about babies being thrown out of train windows and the like. My parents schooled us on the things deemed most important to them, and I internalized those values. If I was worried about something they considered trivial, they would say, "That's ridiculous. Don't worry about that. Worry about something more important!" If my father thought I was spending too much time playing dolls with a neighbor girl, he would say, "Enough already with the dolls, that's *narishkeit* [foolishness]. Go read a book!" When I was in about fourth grade, I had the genius idea to pick wildflowers and sell them to our neighbors. When my father got wind of this, he made me go door to door returning the money I'd made. Ours was not a household where my dad would spend a lazy afternoon playing catch with my brother. Instead, my father wanted him to devote his time to learning Hebrew and studying Talmud.

And yet there were moments of levity. At some point during my high school years, the big news around town was that Senator Ted Kennedy was coming to Gardner. In the weeks leading up to this event, I'd entertain my family by pretending that he was a guest at our dinner table. I'd say things like, "Oh, Teddy, how are you this evening?" and, "Thank you so much for coming." Years later, when Joe was in the Senate, I shared this story with Ted Kennedy, who was equally amused. Another high school memory: a costume party held in my family's garage. My mother, dressed as a geisha, was in her element, passing trays of food and making small talk. Unlike my father, she loved to be the center of attention.

Did I ever rebel? Not really. I remember hiding a bag full of clothes when I left the house so I could change out of the more conservative ones my parents deemed suitable. And there was the unfortunate incident on the day of my high school graduation. I was driving the family car around town, a feeling of elation coursing through my hands as I gripped the steering wheel. I would be leaving Gardner soon and daydreamed about the possibilities for the next chapter of my life. Whipping around the town's tree-lined avenues, my mind was more focused on my rosy future than on the road. Suddenly I was jolted out of my reverie with a literal bang: I had run right into a tree. Fortunately, I was not hurt, but there was a big dent in the side door of my parents' car.

I rushed to a nearby garage, whose local mechanics had repaired my family's cars for years. "I'm graduating today, and I just crashed my dad's car," I told them in a panic. "You've got to help me!" Not only was it my graduation, but as head of the city's Interfaith Ministerial Alliance, my father was giving the baccalaureate prayer at the ceremony. I could envision his face if I showed up in a smashed-up car. It would ruin the occasion. I'd had it drummed into me: "You have to be good and set an example because Daddy is the rabbi." Luckily, I hadn't done any real damage, and they were able to hammer out the dent quickly.

As I got older, my mother would tell me about American athletes who had bought new homes for their mothers. She loved hearing those stories. I never did get to buy them a home, but I was able to help them in many other ways—a tiny payback for all they gave me. For my parents, as they often said, my success in the world was all the payback they ever wanted. They were not materialistic people in any way. My mother told me that what made her life worthwhile was that I was happy. Later, after they retired, they gave me a priceless gift: they moved near me in Riverdale, New York, so they could help take care of my son, Ethan. We thought of gifts in a different way. And, for us, *America* was the greatest gift of all.

Flash-forward to the frenetic activities of the 2000 vice-presidential campaign. One thing that stands out from that time were the reactions from other immigrants. Out on the campaign trail, people would eagerly tell me how *they* came to this country. Each tale was unique, but they all shared a universal quality—the immigrant's story—that connected them in a profound way to each other and to me. There was the man who emigrated from Zimbabwe and became a university professor; the family who had taken a boat from Cambodia to escape war; a woman from Guatemala who cleaned houses to put her children through college—and they were doing beautifully and making her proud. These are perhaps the most American stories of all, and need to be told widely. I felt a strong kinship with these hardworking people. They were dreamers, an accurate term for most immigrants!

I am deeply touched to be seen as a role model for any immigrants who find in my story a connection to their own past or present struggles—and can perhaps see in it the promise of their own future and that of their children and grandchildren.

My brother, who was born in this country, often tells me that I am still too much of an immigrant—too much the child of Holocaust survivors. Though I understand his feelings, I take pride in my past and consider my very presence in the United States to be a victory over evil. My life, my work, and, most important, all that I have taught my children are testaments to my parents and our history.

FOUR

Leaving Gardner

The world breaks everyone and afterward many
are strong at the broken places.

Ernest Hemingway | *A Farewell to Arms*

Having grown up in a home with limited financial resources, working for what I wanted or needed was never in question. I had to.
Other than in childhood, when my father put bread on the table,
I have never been totally supported by a man. In both of my marriages, I was always a financial partner. A two-income household
is the norm today, but back then many women were stay-at-home
wives and mothers. I am proud of my professional accomplishments
as well as the financial contributions I have made.

My work experience began as it does for many girls—as a babysit-
ter. Please don't ask what we were paid then; it is shocking in comparison to the $15 to $20 an hour many young people get today. From
high school and into college, I spent my summers as a counselor at
Camp Young Judaea in New Hampshire, not far from Gardner. Before college, I made extra money doing secretarial work at Yeshiva
University in New York City. I stayed at my aunt's house in Brooklyn
and commuted to the job. The subways were always delayed, and I
had a boss who gave me a hard time if I was five or ten minutes late.
I can still hear her admonishing me, "Work starts at 9:00, not 9:10."

I had originally hoped to major in international studies at Boston University, but when I toured the campus with my father and he saw couples sitting close together in a student lounge, he said, "You don't need that." He wanted me to go to Stern College, the women's college of Yeshiva University, for two years and "adjust to that lifestyle," by which I think he meant I should concentrate on my studies and not "major in boys." If I still wanted to transfer to Boston University after that, he promised I could. And that is what happened.

At BU I decided to major in Chinese studies. I'd become fascinated by Chairman Mao and wanted to learn more about how this massive Communist society functioned. Since I enjoyed acting, I minored in theater. In fact, one of the things I had done at Stern was to appear in a production of *Man and Superman* at the Bowery Lane, an off-Broadway theater. It was a wonderful experience. My father read George Bernard Shaw's script prior to seeing the show and complained that it was too long. After sitting through the production with my mother, he said, "You need a pillow, it's so long." I didn't know he was a theater critic! But he was right: it was too long. As usual, my father had an opinion, especially about anything related to me. I took part in other student plays too. I did not become an actress, but being comfortable on stage certainly came in handy in later life.

In 1970 I received a BA from Boston University, where I majored in government and dramatics. After that I went to Northeastern University, where I received an MA in international relations. In my senior year at BU, I went to Harvard for Shabbat services. That was where I met Gordon Tucker, who was a year behind me in school. We were married a year after he graduated, on the hottest day of the summer in a shul in Leominster that didn't have air-conditioning. Not many people had central air back then, but our guests were not too happy about the heat.

After we married, Gordon and I moved to Washington Heights in Manhattan. He was studying at the Jewish Theological Seminary to become a rabbi as well as pursuing a PhD in logic at Princeton. It was up to me to support us while Gordon was in school. My job hunt took place during an economic downturn when it was no easy task to secure an interview, let alone employment. Eventually I landed a job as a consumer analyst at Lehman Brothers. Basically, I worked as an assistant who researched stocks.

There I was in this beautiful office on Wall Street, but it was a long way from the friendly small town of my youth. In Gardner there was a neighborliness to people, who all knew each other, more or less. And Boston, where I'd spent the last few years, was an equally welcoming place, swarming with like-minded young people. I was shocked, my first day at Lehman, at how cold everyone was. When I had previously lived in the city, I had led the cocooned life of an undergraduate. This was before the age of computers, so people were not hiding behind their monitors. Nonetheless, when I walked through the office, hardly anyone made eye contact or even looked up from their desks.

It was a different time then. Some restaurants, for example, had sections that did not seat women, so when my company was hosting a lunch meeting in mixed company, it had to take place in the "women's" section.

I will never forget when I was chastised for making a mistake at work. My supervisor was furious. "You are going to close us down for what you did," he chided. I thought my career was over before it really began. Luckily, my mistake did not close Lehman Brothers down (that happened many years later without my help). In time I became a full-fledged consumer goods analyst, but in truth, that job—and Wall Street—was not a good fit for me. Nevertheless, working at Lehman Brothers was a good thing to have on my résumé as a career starter.

I'm sure it helped me get my second job, which was more to my liking: I was hired to work in the Public Affairs and Planning Division of Hoffmann–La Roche, an international health care and pharmaceutical company based in Nutley, New Jersey. As part of my job, I initiated a series of seminars on Capitol Hill focusing on such critical issues as recombinant DNA research and national health insurance. Gordon and I were still living in Washington Heights, and the company sent a van for a group of us who were coming from the area and various parts of New Jersey. Then we moved to Riverdale in the Bronx after I gave birth to my first child, Ethan, in order to have more space. Many women in the workforce at that time quit their jobs once they had a child, but that was never an option for me. It meant, for example, that a friend would drive us to a grocery store during our lunch hour so we could shop. At the end of the day, I'd schlep the bags from her car to the van that took me back to Riverdale. Many Thursday nights I'd be cooking until 2:00 a.m. because there wouldn't be time to do it after I came home from work the next day, even though I always had an arrangement to leave early on Fridays so that I would not have to travel once the Sabbath started.

While many working parents today drop off their children at day care, the norm in the 1970s among many was to employ a caretaker in the home. The interview process could be nerve-wracking, and I know I'm not the only parent with horror stories. One woman I interviewed turned out to have an alias; I was so unnerved by the situation that I ended up changing our phone number. In fact, I found someone who had good references and was loving and capable. She was a devout Christian but understood *kashrut* (the Jewish dietary laws) and kept Ethan on a firm schedule. One time my mother came for a visit and the caregiver wouldn't wake up the baby, even for his grandmother. My mother was not too happy about that!

Knowing that my baby was well tended made it easier for me to focus on my work, but it wasn't easy. My mother would chastise me, saying I spent too much time at the office. But I had no choice. In addition, the commute was taxing, and I wanted to work in the city. Luckily, a job came up with Pfizer Pharmaceuticals on West

Forty-Second Street, where I stayed from 1982 to 1985 as director of policy planning and communications. Among other initiatives, I directed the launch of an $11 million health care education campaign.

I was in a good place professionally, but things on the home front were not rosy: Gordon and I were living separately and were in the process of getting divorced. Reflecting on divorce is particularly difficult because it is so personal; every divorce is uniquely challenging. There is, however, a common denominator: the pain it causes everyone involved.

Divorce charged into my life. For a traditional woman like myself, it was an unwelcome interloper in the life I had planned, but I could not let it become an insurmountable foe. The process was not easy. During the early days of the separation, I felt lost. Certainly this was not the script I would have written for myself when I was a little girl—like that of many others, mine included a happy marriage and children. But there are many things in life that are not in our control and things G-d has planned for us that are also not in our understanding but can ultimately prove beneficial beyond what we might imagine.

I was twenty-four when I met my first husband. An ambitious, optimistic young woman, I had big dreams of making important contributions to the world. I also wanted to start a family. Meeting an equally ambitious young man whose dream was to become a rabbi and with whom I shared the same values made our union seem like a perfect fit. We got married and then had a darling son whom we both adored. Giving my parents a grandchild was amazing; a gift they never thought they would receive after the awful times they had been through. Things seemed to be going the way they were supposed to, but gradually over time, Gordon and I had to face a difficult truth: we had grown apart.

Divorce, the great leveling experience of our time, exacts its toll, demanding readjustment and adaptation. What was most painful for me was its unpredictability. Suddenly, at age thirty and with a three-year-old son, I had joined the ranks of women who had become divorcees, a club in which I never thought I'd become a member. The irony is that the process of divorce is like an out-of-control train bearing down on you, but at the same time, it is you driving the train. In its early stages especially, divorce for me was more devastating than an illness.

In my traditional home with two Holocaust survivor parents, divorce wasn't a subject that was ever broached. My immigrant family always stressed resilience in the face of hardship. If two people didn't get along, they didn't get divorced; they just toughed it out. In our circle it was considered a *shanda*—Yiddish for a shameful thing.

Everything in my upbringing reinforced the idea that divorce could never be an appropriate response. My parents had survived the greatest evil the world had known, so who was I to complain about a less-than-perfect marriage? Surely I could make it work! I was charged with fighting greater battles than those that existed in the realm of the personal. At first, that was how I felt and how I talked to myself in the dark of night. Over time, however, I began to realize that this line of thinking failed to account for the fact that I had to be true to myself. I had to take care of myself in order to take care of others, including my son and parents. Once I internalized this idea, I was able to accept the necessity of divorce.

What had previously been unthinkable became the only healthy course of action. *So it happened.* Over the years, people have asked me for details or to speculate why my first marriage did not succeed. There is no reason to do that. It was not a dramatic denouement. Rather, two nice people came to a crossroads and chose to walk down separate paths.

Like many other women of my age, I was influenced by feminist literature. I was among that early group that was feminist but didn't label ourselves as such. We knew we needed to get educated and work hard and to be more forward about getting equal rights. But I wasn't fighting for equal rights per se; I was just learning from Betty

Friedan, Gloria Steinem, Germaine Greer, and so many other pioneering women. They were talking to us through books and lectures, television and radio, about the importance of women and our independent role in society. I was living it.

My parents' encouragement was never gender based. My mother, in particular, didn't think feminism was helpful to women. It just wasn't on her radar. Both parents championed my ambitions and achievements as much as they did my brother Ary's. They never made me feel "less than" because I was female.

But divorce was different. It wasn't something that was considered an appropriate response in any circumstance. Initially, and understandably, my parents counseled me not to rush—because of my son and because of my marriage itself. Their message was to try harder and see if my husband and I could work it out. We tried, but eventually my parents came to the realization that even with time, our marriage wasn't going to work.

I began adjusting to my new reality by asking questions. Perhaps the most important question was: What do I tell my son? How do you tell your children without destroying their faith in the sanctity of marriage, their own safe future, or the other parent? The failure of a marriage is a shattering experience for everyone involved, but it is the responsibility of parents to remain strong for their children in the face of such immense pain.

Ethan was so young at the time, but I knew that my conduct then could have an impact on the rest of his life. I was determined to be a positive role model for him. This is not to say that I did not succumb to emotion. Many days I went into the bathroom and cried into a towel. I used to put an "X" on the calendar for every day I went without breaking down in tears. After a month or so with fewer Xs, it became a little easier to smile for my son, even if I didn't feel like it.

People often say that divorce is much harsher and more complicated when there are children involved. That is true, but in my case, Ethan provided a common bond between me and my ex-husband.

Any pettiness or squabbles were immediately put into perspective due to the fact that we were accountable to our son. Our duty to him superseded all other concerns. How incredible it is that simply looking at a toddler can let you know exactly what needs to be done.

I am also a big fan of taking a time-out in any emotionally fraught situation, which I discovered can work wonders. For some time after the divorce, I hid behind a mask that indicated everything was fine. When it became clear that this wasn't working—inside, I was still reeling—I told myself, *You are going to take yourself to Miami Beach for a relaxing, meditative weekend.* And that is exactly what I did. I flew to Miami and checked into a hotel. However, when I opened the door to my room, it was small and uncomfortable and made me feel more depressed. I called the desk and told them I was checking out. To me, it was a moment of assertion that I mattered and would not accept less than what I wanted.

On a whim, I asked a guy in the lobby, "What's a good hotel around here?" He replied, "The Fontainebleau." Not realizing it was one of the swankiest hotels in the area, I took a cab there. In the lobby, I happened to meet a group of men and women from Manhattan and started chatting with them. It was refreshing to feel like a person again—an independent woman living life on my own terms, albeit briefly. That evening, as I looked out at the Atlantic Ocean, I felt my sense of self returning.

Yet questions persisted in my mind, especially those surrounding faith: Why is this happening to me? G-d, are you listening to me? What do you have in mind for me in the years ahead? The foundation that I built my life on was crumbling. Paradoxically, I felt as though I had let G-d down in some way, as though I was rebuking what is holy.

Attending synagogue services after the separation was strange. I had been my father's daughter, then my husband's wife. Now I was Hadassah. I had to realize that wasn't a bad thing. In fact, it was a beautiful and powerful thing. I began to understand myself in previously undiscovered ways. I meditated on my parents' experience—how they had remained resilient and committed to community, faith, and prosperity when they had every right to slip into anger and hate. Using their example, I entered into a new compact with G-d. In the aftermath of my marriage, I realized something that has stayed with me to this day: that the possibilities of the future are more endless and positive than are the difficulties of the past. The future was something I held in my own hands. It was heavy with responsibility but also full of opportunity. Whatever direction my life would take was up to me, and me alone. My parents were survivors in the truest sense of the word, and now I was too, although in a very different way.

Rebuilding was a collective effort, a process in which my father was instrumental. As I have said, my father was a man who believed in moving forward. In the midst of my early questioning and grief, he told me, "You have to look at your marriage like it's a shattered vase. You are trying to put it back together, but it may not be possible." I had to accept the fact that *that* vase was shattered and I needed to move forward for myself and my son.

Regardless of my parents' initial concerns, they chose pragmatism over judgment and stepped in to help, especially with Ethan as I shared parenting with his father. My father picked Ethan up at after school, and they sang songs on the way home, where my mother had snacks waiting for them. With your parents, you don't want to be a kid again, but sometimes you just have to be thankful for the support system they provide. I was lucky: they saw the future in Ethan and gave selflessly, as always, to ensure the protection of that future.

As anyone who has been divorced knows, there is no shortage of impediments to overcome. Social, religious, emotional, and financial barriers seem to erect themselves out of thin air. Thankfully, after our divorce was finalized, my ex-husband and I remained civil. But that did not take away from the fact that my life had been radically altered. The world I found myself living in was a frightening, foreign place. I could either let this new reality overwhelm me, or I could adapt to it. I don't have to tell you what option I chose; I am, after all, my parents' daughter.

But I won't deny that I was lonely and hurting. I tried to fortify myself by following the basics: exercising regularly—I found solace in the pool—eating right, taking vitamins, and trying not to get too worked up when things invariably didn't go as planned. Easier said than done, for sure. Aside from work, I tried to keep busy as much as possible, though I remember how quiet the house felt on Sunday mornings when Ethan was with his father. My brother was a constant support during this time, as was a work friend of mine, an attorney who had a baby a month after I did.

Although my life was headed in the right direction, my heart felt incomplete. I had a desire to reconnect with the world on an intimate level but had no idea how to go about doing so. And I didn't know if I could allow myself to fall in love again. It was hard to believe that it could last. Even after you pick up the pieces, you still have to contend with the fact that the vase had broken. Who is to say you won't break another one?

Something else terrified me more: the idea that I would let fear win. It took time, but eventually I was able to allow for the possibility of love reentering my life. I am so glad I did.

I would be remiss if I didn't share a few more pieces of pragmatic advice. If you are going through a divorce, it is inevitable that gossip will enter your life. Pay it no mind. People may try to probe, for many reasons. Unless a person is close to you, it's none of their business why you got a divorce or even "how things are going." Limit yourself, even when you want to vent. Every word not spoken in a moment of emotion is precious. You don't owe anybody anything. This is your struggle, not theirs.

It is also important to remember that with a situation as difficult as divorce, there is no rulebook, no single response. If you ask me what the single best thing that someone going through it should do, I will tell you there is no single best thing. But whatever your strategy, it is imperative that you work at it. You must dedicate yourself to your new path with even more vigor and hopefulness than you put into your marriage. This is not a drill; this is your life. Do not succumb to the notion that you are broken or unworthy. Prove your own worth to yourself every day.

> Pain can make us moody and bitter at the world, withdrawn, hard to be with, supercritical. In the best case it becomes a means of understanding the suffering of others. Through our own pain we can learn how others feel who likewise suffer. In that way adversity may have a wholesome effect. The secret to overcoming it is not to *do* much, but to *be* much, and moreover, to realize that being is more than having. In fact, *being* is the only thing in life that is truly worthwhile.
>
> Rabbi Samuel Freilich | from a sermon in Gardner, Massachusetts, spring 1970

Surviving divorce takes a great deal of maturity and also generosity—toward yourself, toward the person you are divorcing, as well as all the family and friends who were part of your married life and will now play different roles to which they too must become accustomed. Don't make every holiday, every gathering uncomfortable for them. Divorce is hard enough; don't exacerbate it.

Finally, remember that we are all so much stronger than we think we are. Thanks to G-d (as I like to express it in Hebrew, *Baruch Hashem*) and to the people who love us, the winds of change can blow us into a whole new and wonderful place. If divorce becomes unavoidable, you must focus on moving forward with your life and not view this as a failure.

FIVE

Remarriage, Motherhood, and Meaning

With a new day comes new strength and new thoughts.

Eleanor Roosevelt

Remarriage is the greatest surprise of all. To fall in love, to marry again, to pledge forever seems incredulous when considering my not-so-distant past. When I first met Joe Lieberman, I had been divorced for about a year and wasn't looking for love. I had gone out on dates from time to time, but only with men who were also fathers. Life was hectic. Commuting from Riverdale to my job at Pfizer in Manhattan, I was focused on tending to Ethan and excelling at work, and I was still dealing with my feelings about the divorce. Then my friend Edie Goldberg told me there was someone she wanted me to meet. He was "a very nice man in her synagogue in New Haven." As an inducement, she said, "Ethan looks like him." Edie and I were close as close could be; she had been my roommate during our freshman and sophomore years of college. I trusted her, and something in her voice let me know she was serious. "He's a politician but he seems like a good guy," Edie told me. I still laugh about her qualifying statement.

Two observant Jews meeting on Easter —who would have thought it?

When Joe phoned that morning, I answered the call on the first ring.

"Hi," he began. "It's Joe Lieberman from New Haven."

"Oh, Edie's friend," I replied.

"That's me. Are you free today?"

"Today?"

"Yes. I'm running for attorney general of Connecticut, but there are no political events today because it is Easter Sunday."

"Well that works out perfectly. I just bought a new dining room set, and I need someone to help me move it in." Joe says that line still makes him laugh.

I don't know if he thought I was serious or not, but he drove down from Connecticut to see me. He was a bit tardy. Later he admitted that he had gotten lost on the way because he didn't know the area. The first thing I noticed were his eyes. He looked at me in a way I can't really describe. Clearly there was strong chemistry between us, but I felt something deeper, and I thought he was handsome. Thirty-five years later, I still do.

I was at the Young Israel Synagogue in New Haven when I first heard Hadassah's name. There was a woman there, Edith Goldberg, who as it turned out was Hadassah's college roommate. She came over to me one Sabbath and said, "I have someone I really want to introduce you to, but later." Six months later, I found a little piece of paper on my office desk. There was also a phone number. The note said, "Hadassah Freilich. This is the person I talked to you about. She is worth the trip to New York."

In my single life, I was renting the first-floor apartment in a two-family house that my sister Ellen and brother-in-law Fred owned and lived in. I had already declared my candidacy for attorney general, and now it was Easter Sunday, 1982. Nothing happens in politics on Easter Sunday in Connecticut. With some time on my hands, I found that little note that Edie had left in my office and thought that it might be interesting to go out with a woman named Hadassah. So I called her, and we agreed to meet later that day.

When she opened the door to her apartment and I saw her face for the first time, I thought she was beautiful. Then I went into the kitchen where she had made some kosher food. Her countertops were covered with tin foil because it was Passover. First, I thought this woman was a knockout, and then there she was doing "Kosher for Passover." She was the complete package.

I had found someone very precious.

JOE LIEBERMAN

After our first date, I reckoned, *This is interesting.* He was charming, funny, attractive, and insightful. Still, after my divorce I was extremely protective of myself and my child. Divorce had been unimaginable, so how could I imagine a second husband? And a second husband with *two* children? Even my father had warned me against such leaps of faith. I was reluctant, unwilling to risk what little stability I had been able to create.

Nonetheless, the next weekend I went to New Haven to see Edie. I let Joe know I would be there, and he asked if he could see me on Saturday night. When he picked me up, he told me we would be attending a political event. "If anyone asks, how should I introduce myself?" I said.

"Tell them you're my driver," he replied.

I'm still laughing at that too.

After we left the event—the first of countless ones I would attend with Joe—he took me to a restaurant in New Haven. It must have been near midnight. We started talking about life and about divorce. All of a sudden, the restaurant was closing. Joe suggested we go back to Edie's house, where we talked until three in the morning.

There were hurdles. For starters, we had to figure out how we

ng to date, especially since he was in the middle of a polit-
ɔaign. We realized that he could come down to my apart-
... after his campaigning, stay for a few hours, then drive back. In
the midst of all this, the time came for me to meet Joe's parents and
his sisters, Rietta and Ellen. From the start they were friendly and
welcoming to me. Later, when they met my parents, my mother gave
Joe's parents the greatest compliment, saying they were *ballabatish*,
meaning they were respectable, traditional, and caring. And they
were very supportive of Joe and of our relationship. Joe's father was
concerned about all the driving Joe was doing during our courtship
between New Haven and Riverdale and warned us that such an arrangement would be very difficult to maintain for long. Joe thought
his dad was encouraging us to get engaged soon.

When I met Joe, he was "a fellow who follows a dream," as the
song from *Finian's Rainbow* puts it. His was a noble dream: to serve
the public, using his knowledge of the law and his deep sense of
right and wrong. His mission was to help ensure that our laws, public
policies, and available services were worthy of our democracy; that
they made it possible for people of all backgrounds to be able to
dream big, follow their dreams, and achieve them.

Over time, I saw that his ambition was not to hold public office merely as an end in itself. Rather, it was something that can
be summed up in the Hebrew phrase *tikkun olam*, which means
"repair the world." It is a Jewish concept defined by acts of kindness
performed to improve or even perfect the world.

Joe was not new to politics, having served in the Connecticut
state senate from 1970 to 1980, the last six years as majority leader
for the Democratic party. He had lost a race for US Congress to a
Republican in the 1980 Reagan landslide, but was now hoping to
become state's attorney general.

This was the man I met and fell in love with. While I did "follow
a fellow who follows a dream," my parents had raised me to follow

my own dreams. Joe found and fell in love with an ambitious and determined woman. My dreams were twofold: first, to carry the torch for my parents—meaning to do whatever I could to keep their stories alive, so that the horrors they endured would never be forgotten and would never happen again—and second, as my career objective, to make a difference by educating women about health care, an idea that had taken shape during my years in the workforce.

 Shortly after I met Joe, I had an *aha!* moment in which I knew for sure I was going to be able to let love back into my life. He had come by one Sunday night and played board games with Ethan. After Joe left, Ethan told me, "I like him because he played Monopoly with me. He didn't do it just because of you, but because he likes me."

Such a simple gesture on Joe's part felt good. I saw the possibility of a life that could be profound in its ordinariness. Obviously that is a far cry from how things turned out. No question, the journey Joe and I have taken together is more extraordinary than either of us ever imagined. Nonetheless, when I think about what Joe means to me, I don't think of the political rallies or fancy dinners. What is most extraordinary for me is the comfort of our daily existence.

Love and devotion matter to every part of our lives: not only with our significant other, which is one kind of love, but also with children and grandchildren and in everyday relationships with the people with whom we interact. I will say that the kind of love I share with my husband is what I cherish most. I know that a lot of people don't have it, and that makes me grateful for what I have, sad for what others don't have, and hopeful that they will find the kind of love and friendship that I was so very fortunate to find.

After about seven months of dating, Joe proposed with a small sapphire ring. He wanted to wait until after the election because of all that was going on. He did win that election and would serve as Connecticut's attorney general for six years. A week after he proposed, we announced our engagement to both of our families at a lunch around Thanksgiving 1982 at my apartment in Riverdale. We shared our news over deli platters filled with kosher turkey, salami, and roast beef, as well as mounds of potato salad and coleslaw. Everyone was thrilled. My parents were happy that Joe and I had found each other. They were first and foremost happy that I was happy, and they were confident that we could enrich each other and create a good life together. Then we drove into Manhattan to see *Amadeus* on Broadway. After the play, Joe's Uncle Benny took us to Moshe Peking for a great kosher Chinese dinner.

That was a very special and exciting time. Our wedding was set for March 1983, and there were so many things we had to do. I especially had to work out the logistics of moving up to New Haven. At that point we had three kids: Joe's two, Matt and Becca, and Ethan. We had to look for a house and found one we loved that we bought together. Ethan had to finish the school year in Riverdale, so we began our commute. We enrolled him in a Jewish day school in New Haven for the following September.

We got married in Joe's lovely synagogue in Stamford where his parents lived and was an easy trip for my family and friends who came from New York City. Our three children walked down the aisle—Ethan and Matt on either side of Becca. I turned and smiled when I saw them holding hands and laughing together. Such a lovely moment in a warm and loving affair. Among the guests were Governor William O'Neill of Connecticut and his wife, Nikki. We were honored when Bill, the longest-serving governor in the state's history, toasted us.

After we were married, I left Pfizer. I had to figure out how to best manage my career and my expanded brood while living in New Haven. Ethan, then seven, went to his father's house in the Bronx three weekends a month, another variable to add to the equation. Joe's two teens were in high school. Fortunately, their school was around the corner from our house and close to their mother's place, so they were able to go back and forth between their parents fairly easily. Even with that close proximity, however, there were big adjustments for every one of us.

Most people ask themselves certain fundamental questions: From where do I derive meaning? Where do I belong? How can I find happiness?

We all struggle with these questions. I certainly don't have all the answers, but at the same time, I do know this: my marriage, my children, and my faith are the cornerstones of my happiness. Everyone's journey is different. For me, prioritizing family is the foundation of my sense of self. Again, families might not always look like the so-called traditional family, but the core concept remains unchanged. A family, as my very articulate son Matt says, is built on "shared experiences with the necessity to create bonds."

Similarly, mothers come in all forms: biological, adoptive, blended. Ultimately, the circumstances through which you become a mother are unimportant. What matters is showing up. Being a mother is a lot about *presence*. You have to be ready to give your all to your children. It is inherently rooted in unselfishness: you cease to be the center of your universe in order to build a better one.

Unquestionably, if you are present in your children's lives, all the extraneous stuff will fall by the wayside. They will feel your love for them, your investment in them. Strained bonds will mend. It's the best feeling for a parent to experience.

Welcoming Joe's two children into my life expanded my idea of motherhood. I had to create a space for them in my heart that was as large as the one I had for Ethan. There were times I heard Matt and Becca grouse about me to their father, and I held my tongue. I understood what they were struggling with, and as painful as it was, I would not put Joe in the position of being caught in the middle, having to hear complaints from both his children and his new wife.

I don't know that parents really understand how tough divorce is on their kids—unless they too are children of divorce. Even if the marriage was not good and everyone is better off in some ways, there was still a sense of security lost and a conflict about loyalties too. Moving between my parents' homes was difficult. We moved from one to the other every week on Sundays and Wednesdays, to start. Everyone would say, "Your parents love you so much, they want you to be with them as much as possible." That may be so, but they didn't look beyond their needs to consider what it was like for us to constantly move and to pack and unpack.

Everything became more complicated when my father married Hadassah. I really liked Hadassah from the beginning, but I resented the attention she got from my dad and the partnership she had with him. In time, and with great understanding and patience on Hadassah's part, it all improved. I know now that what Hadassah did was put her feelings aside, which was an act of selflessness. I truly love and respect her today beyond what words can express.

BECCA LIEBERMAN

I also understood that it was painful for them to see the attention that their father gave to my son. Ethan went from being an only child to having two new siblings who had entered our private world. He wanted them to like and accept him, but that was hard at first. He was a wise little boy, and I believe he understood it would take time. Thank G-d, all our children, now parents themselves, are as close as siblings can be.

Hadassah's mom grew up with a point of view and understanding of life that includes the large reality of suffering. As a result, Hadassah does not hold to the idea that somehow everyone deserves to have a happy and easy life at all times. The fact that things between us were difficult in the beginning was not as daunting to her as it could have been to other people. She made a point of describing how bad other people's situations were, and that we should count ourselves as lucky. At the same time, she pointed out that we should also make sure we never ended up like that out of our own doing.

From a kid's perspective, it was a little annoying, but now I see it as a valuable insight. It's not your typical happy message, but it was actually a helpful message.

Matt Lieberman

One of my cardinal rules in those early days, and throughout my remarriage, was that I would never, under any circumstance, speak one negative word about Matt and Becca's mother or Ethan's father. Bad-mouthing a parent to children or saying negative things within their earshot can lead to confusion, resentment, and guilt—and for something that is never their fault. This can make them even more insecure and fill them with self-doubt, wondering, *Did our parents ever love each other? If not, what does that say about me?*

When recalling a relationship with a former spouse, many find it difficult to honestly describe that relationship. We have to acknowledge that a "first"—a first love, a first marriage, a first child—has its own magic. There's a tendency to push the positive reminiscences of that "first" aside as we focus on the present and the future. Yet if children are a product of that "first," it is important to revel in those reminiscences so that we acknowledge the part those offspring played in that "first" too.

Though Joe and I both had children from our first marriages, the word *step* does not exist in our vocabulary. Matt, Becca, Ethan, and Hani are our children. We made a conscious decision not to use that word. Accepting each member of our blended family and verbalizing them as full children, not as a step- or even half-brother or half-sister, made a critical difference to us. I consider this my greatest accomplishment: creating a fully integrated, tightly knit, and loving family.

When you marry, you are saying to each other: "I will always love and honor what's yours, and you will always love and honor what's mine." How can a person love you totally unless he or she can also love your children? This may sound easy, but it is not, as so many of us discover. In the process, I had to learn to set aside pride and ego and remain patient and focused on the greater good.

We moved into our beautiful house in the Westville section of New Haven, a mixed neighborhood with people from different walks of life. Some were part of the Orthodox community and had been at our wedding. Others looked at me like, "Who is this person Joe has taken as a wife?" I was learning to be a neighbor and carpooler plus all the other roles we take on in life. Private citizens have a lot more freedom than political figures. There were many "political lessons" I had to learn, with only Joe for a teacher. (These days, political leaders are not quite as restricted in their comments as we used to be.) Being married to a public figure, regardless of the arena, means having to adjust to an accelerated pace and an intense and not always friendly scrutiny. In that regard, the partner will likely find herself or himself having to weather some blistering attacks from time to time. Even when you're told to "not take it personally," you still do. Once in a private setting, I was voicing my opinion on something quite aggressively, and Joe said to me afterward, "Don't say that too loudly because it will be in the *Hartford Courant* tomorrow." I realized that from then on that I had to watch myself. It was a slow but interesting learning process.

Once we were settled, I started looking for a career locally. Eventually I signed on as a policy analyst at Saint Raphael Corporation, the parent company of the Hospital of Saint Raphael. From 1986 to 1988 I worked in its communications department, where I was involved in the company's marketing, planning, public relations, and advertising efforts. The New Haven offices were housed in the nunnery—this was a Catholic institution, after all. One of our initiatives was to educate the public about the significant role nurses play in our health care system, especially in hospitals. This is understood today, but back then nurses were not accorded the same level of respect (or gratitude) that doctors received.

Was everything wonderful and perfect, day in and day out, as Joe and I combined our ambitions, our dreams, our lives? Of course not. It took work, just as everything worth having does. And it took making sacrifices, small and large, and sometimes putting Joe's needs ahead of my own. Joe and I have had our difficult days like everyone else. Believe me, the scrutiny of a national political campaign can introduce stress into the healthiest of relationships. Through it all, though, I always felt that I had someone who believed in me and loved me, and I know Joe feels the same, because it is true.

Like most other people, I sometimes question my choices, always trying to make the right ones. But when I fell in love with Joe, there was never a doubt about my choice. It may seem absurd to say that another person is all it takes to make you happy. Nonetheless, meeting Joe did just that, and more, for me. I believe that is because he is not "another" person, a separate entity, from me, but rather in so many ways an extension of me—someone who has helped me find myself in ways I had never done before. In sharing a life with Joe Lieberman, I understood the full import of Plato's famous quote about two halves seeking and finding each other. Joe has always had a calming effect on me because he is the most reasonable person I have ever met. I tend to be impulsive and not much of a long-range planner. For my part, I think I added some excitement and color to his life. It's a good balance.

Joe and I wanted to have a child together. We knew this would not be easy. There were several medical challenges I had to deal with, including getting help from a fertility doctor. Once again, I have to say *Baruch Hashem*, because in addition to modern medicine, I know there was a divine hand in this, and I became pregnant.

One day in 1987, when I was two months pregnant and we had not revealed this information to anyone, we were sitting with Stan Greenberg, who was then on the political science faculty at Yale. Serving as Joe's pollster, he was advising us and our campaign manager, Sherry Brown, on Joe's possible run for the US Senate. Not knowing the private drama of my pregnancy, Stan said with a smile: "Hadassah, if we do this and you really want to help the campaign, you'll have a baby." A few months later, we joked with Stan that we had taken his advice to heart.

I was pregnant during the entire Senate campaign, crisscrossing the state for countless fundraising events, meet-and-greets, and diner stops. It was exciting and exhausting. In addition to the Senate race and my pregnancy, I decided that now was the time to enable my father to fulfill his dream of completing the English translation and publication of his memoir, *The Coldest Winter*. My parents still lived in Riverdale. My father had just begun to suffer from Parkinson's. He would come up and stay at our house to work on the book with a local writer, Joseph Berg, who knew Yiddish. They would sit at our kitchen table, translating my father's words. He would complain that the effort was wiping him out, though from watching my father work, I knew he was pleased with the process. I told Joe, "Thank G-d we found this wonderful man."

What a year that was! The book was completed and published and, on March 15, 1988, our daughter Hani—one of the greatest blessings of my life—was born. She helped to link our family together. Hani was a common touchstone for all of us, a biological bridge that made all of our ties infinitely stronger. That November, Joe was elected to the US Senate, a position he held for twenty-four years.

When my sister Hani was born, it definitely added a positive dynamic in our family. But even before that, things had settled down. From the perspective of so many years that have passed, having Becca and Matt as my sister and brother is one of the greatest blessings ever. We could not be closer. Having to live with and adjust to your parents' divorce and remarriage is difficult under any circumstance. I think a large part of the reason things worked out so well for us is that my mom handled their temporary teenage dismissive behavior toward her with such grace and love.

Rabbi Ethan Tucker

My mother did a great job of "blending" a family. She had to make that a priority. It's a lesson for life in general: you have priorities and goals that are at the center of whatever you're doing, and they help you navigate the day-to-day issues. I was the glue in the family that helped create a cohesive unit among the siblings. Ethan didn't share parents with Becca and Matt, and Becca and Matt didn't share parents with Ethan. All shared a parent with me.

HANI LIEBERMAN

There's a whole set of conflicts and frustrations that came up with living in a house with different rules and habits. But at a certain point, anger just takes too much energy. I realized there was work to be done to make our family truly connected and that it was going to require a new level of maturity and generosity from me.

Once someone asked me if I minded that Hadassah called me her daughter. My answer, without hesitation, was, "Of course not." I *am* her daughter and will always be. Hani was a huge part of that. We all used her as a focal point to grow around, and it worked. She was just such brightness in our lives during a time when we all needed it. She made us a whole new family.

Now, looking back on it, I can see what a large role Hadassah played in that process. She was always so patient with us, emphasizing the things that mattered while still making the small concerns of our lives feel important. And Hani was her gift to us.

BECCA LIEBERMAN

If I had to say only one thing about family, it would be this: approach it without fear. Some people falsely believe that an emphasis on family will constrain them and take away their individuality. In fact, it's just the opposite. I've never felt freer than when I lay my head next to Joe's, or when I tuck my children, and now grandchildren, into bed, or when I attend an event of importance to them. There is great satisfaction in seeing my children grow up, seeing them help their communities and the world at large. And don't even get me started on the joys of being a grandparent to my twelve beloved children's children! Because my grandparents died before I was born, I never experienced the special bond that can form between a grandparent and a grandchild. In truth, when I was young, I didn't appreciate what I was missing. How could I? It wasn't the norm at my parents' home to set a large table for the extended family. So how could I feel the absence of something I had never experienced? I suppose in certain ways, my Aunt Rozi, my mother's sister, fulfilled that role in my life. She was always so accepting of me, offering unconditional support and never questioning any of my choices. When I visited her when I was attending Stern College in New York City, an array of cooked dishes would be cooling on the windowsill, waiting to be wrapped and hauled back to my dormitory room. How different things are for my own grandchildren: I relish my role in their lives and never take it for granted.

My father, G-d rest his soul, taught me a lot about being a parent. He was never afraid to speak his mind. So many parents today are reluctant to tell their child what to do. More important, they often don't guide them with a firm hand in terms of their education. That fearful or hesitant mind-set is alien to me. I am not encouraging any-one to be a "helicopter parent," always hovering, overly involved or controlling. As they grow up, children need to be able to sort things out for themselves and even make some mistakes on their own. That is how they learn. But my father did not hesitate to chastise me when it came to bad behavior or if he didn't like what I was wearing. I'd be afraid I wouldn't have a bed that night if I didn't listen to him. There is some real wisdom in that: children need leadership from their parents, not friendship.

My son Matt recently told me something that made me laugh and also contained a great deal of truth. "You did a really good job of conveying two things," he said. "One, that we were one family and that we were 'all in it together.' And, two, given what your parents had experienced on a catastrophic scale—things could always be worse." The takeaway for Matt was that while the world is a dan-gerous place, counting your blessings and staying close to those you hold dear is a powerful way to navigate through the obstacles that life puts in our way.

I am proud to say that this philosophy, especially "staying close to those you hold dear," has helped Joe and me raise our children to become amazing adults with solid values, noteworthy accomplishments, and a strong sense of themselves as people who have a rich heritage to carry on. I am not minimizing the important roles that Ethan's father and Matt and Becca's mother have played. But I'd like to think that our four children were also influenced by our long-standing commitment to civic engagement and public service. In fact, each of our children has internalized this belief and, in his or her own way, has contributed to the greater good. They are following their dreams and have found success and happiness in their families and chosen professions. What more could a parent ask for?

My divorce and remarriage are topics I have always been very private about. In writing this book, though, I felt an obligation to help other people by opening up about subjects I would have never discussed publicly before. Statistics show that many remarriages don't work, often because the children involved don't like what they see or feel. That could have happened to us too. Of course, it's easier to talk about things from this vantage point. Nonetheless, Joe and I are appreciative of how blessed we are that things turned out as they did for us and our children.

six Living in the Spotlight

*When I dare to be powerful—to use my strength in the service of my vision—
then it becomes less and less important whether I am afraid.*

Audre Lorde | author and civil rights activist

I have had a sense of duty for as long I can remember, instilled in me
by my father, a rabbi who led a congregation, and by my mother, a
survivor who guided a family. As the English novelist George Eliot
famously asked, "What do we live for if not to make life less difficult
for each other?"

Living as though we can make a difference is important—because we can. Small actions eventually add up to big changes in
whatever the cause is. My personal civic service has always been
rooted in a deep appreciation for America and the ideals for which
it stands. I believe that we must commit ourselves to bettering our
communities, fighting injustice wherever we see it, and, especially
meaningful for me, finding the best ways to extend the American
experience to immigrants.

The opportunities I have had in America mean everything to
me. They mean liberation from fascism. They mean furthering
the dream of equality. That's why I, as one individual, believe in
and work for more positive possibilities for all. Public service does
present challenges for which nothing can fully prepare you. Anyone
who has ventured into the public eye, especially in this Internet age,

knows that criticism and sometimes vilification are a certainty. You lose your privacy. But my religion and my family taught me it was worth it.

My marriage to Joe deepened my commitment to public service. Our personal relationship opened up more avenues for me to help people. It afforded me access to the inner workings of our government, access that grew as Joe ascended the political ladder. It was thrilling to be part of a team that truly believed it could change this country for the better. I also believe my parents' background, and my own status as an immigrant who became a naturalized citizen, had a big effect on Joe. He will tell you that it made him even more understanding and committed to the principles that form the bedrock of both our lives and of America. It made him more sensitive to the complex and compelling issues of immigration as well.

When Joe was sworn in as a senator, our entire family came. We all stayed at the Willard InterContinental, a beautifully renovated old hotel on Pennsylvania Avenue, steps from the White House. Between our families—parents, cousins, siblings, aunts, uncles—we took up nearly an entire floor. It was a difficult trip for my father, now in a wheelchair, but there was no way he would miss it. Joe's mother was there to celebrate her son and honor the memory of his father, who had died two years before. Having everyone together that day felt momentous, as though the American dreams of two different families were being realized simultaneously.

I was seated with my mother and father in the lobby of the Willard, waiting to head over to the Senate, when Senator Paul Simon of Illinois approached us and offered his congratulations. My mother thanked him. He smiled at her and said, "Behind every great man is a surprised mother-in-law." That brought forth a peal of laughter from my mother. Imagine that, a woman who narrowly escaped the Holocaust was now sharing jokes with a senator! It seemed to me at the time, and even now, to encapsulate the promise of this country.

Several weeks before this, there was an orientation program for new senators, during which Joe and I were given the opportunity to go into the Senate chamber. I saw a look of reverence on his face and asked him what he was thinking. "I'm just thinking that here I am in the middle of history," he replied. "Here I am in this special place where so many great people I admire have served. And now I have the opportunity to serve."

Then he looked at me and asked, "And you?"

I looked around, and a feeling of elation washed over me. "I'm thinking of my fist in the air toward Hitler," I told him. "I am thinking, *Here I am. I made it. My family made it.*"

A little more than a month later, on January 3, 1989, Joe went up to the dais of the Senate chamber to take his oath. I knew he wasn't speaking those sacred words just for himself, for me, or for our family watching from their seats in the balcony. He was saying them for all the people he represented. Though I have often been proud of him, there are only a few other times when my pride was stronger than in that moment.

It had taken a while to adjust to the news that he'd won. We thought it might happen, hoped it would happen, but didn't quite believe it was possible—and then it happened. In truth, all the trappings of the victory—endless phone calls, flowers, telegrams, express mail packages—combined to make me feel claustrophobic. It was so enveloping that it was hard to find the time to savor the victory.

Joe initially stayed in a borrowed apartment in DC. As it happened, Alan McFarland, a friend of his from Yale and husband of K. T. McFarland, the foreign policy expert, called Joe right after he won the Senate race and said that K. T.'s apartment was empty and we could stay there until we found our own place. Joe moved into that borrowed apartment in January, and it was a big help. I remember Chris Dodd telling Joe that we should get ourselves a "real home" in DC. He added, "Hadassah must move to Washington. You are going to be there more than you think you are. If she is in Connecticut and you are here a big part of every week, it won't be good for your marriage." We took that advice to heart. I didn't want to be one of those wives whose husband commuted to work in another city. I know it's an arrangement that is tolerable for some couples, but I didn't think it would work for me. While we understood there would be certain weeknights when circumstances would keep us apart, we always tried to be together for Shabbat.

> After one of my campaigns for the Senate, Hadassah and I were both exhilarated but exhausted. After traveling the state, thanking the people throughout Connecticut for the enormous opportunity they had just given me, I needed private time. I needed to be alone with Hadassah and away from the public, even briefly, as much as or probably more than she did. The truth is that I am at least as dependent on her support as she is on mine. That means that I don't like it when we are forced to be apart.
>
> JOE LIEBERMAN

We kept our lovely home in New Haven and went back there about three weekends each month. Six months later, I moved to DC with Hani and our au pair, and we bought a townhouse there. Ethan went to high school at the Ramaz Hebrew Day School in Manhattan, so he was temporarily living with his father during the week and spent most weekends with us. The older two were already embarking on their adult lives but visited as often as they could. I don't want to gloss over the hard parts: one of Joe's colleagues warned that he would be going back and forth between Connecticut and DC so much that some nights he might may not be sure where he was. Moving to DC meant living even farther away from my aging parents, Ethan, Matt, and Becca and the life Joe and I had built together in New Haven. It meant learning our way around an unfamiliar city, understanding what life inside the Beltway was all about, settling in and making new friends. It meant endless scheduling conflicts, rearranging sitters, playdates, doctor appointments, work meetings and lunch dates, and many nights of single parenthood—but it comes with the territory. People were always courteous to us because of Joe's position, but there were some who were genuinely warm and caring and helped to ease our way. Our neighbors, Lisa and Gerard Leval, became dear friends, sharing carpooling duties and treating Hani like their fourth daughter. My friend Mariella Trager was a great resource for everything from recommending the best greengrocer and reasonably priced drycleaner to introducing us to the international community based in DC.

Joe and I understood that we were not a typical Senate couple. He was the only person in the history of the Senate to observe Shabbat. For those of us who are traditionally Sabbath observant, it is a day of rest, meaning doing nothing that qualifies as disrupting G-d's creation, from driving a car to using a phone to turning on the lights. Although Joe never actively engaged in politics on Shabbat, he always believed that he had to fulfill his basic government responsibilities seven days a week, including the relatively rare occasions when there was voting on a Friday night or Saturday. (This is similar to how observant Jewish physicians adapt their religious practice on Shabbat in order to attend to sick patients in their care.) To Joe, there was never a doubt. His personal religious convictions mirrored his approach to serving his country. He did both with commitment to his principles. The private went hand in hand with the public.

We made sure that the house we purchased in Washington was within walking distance of the Senate. That way, if a vote happened on a Friday night or Saturday, Joe could walk there or back home and not break Shabbat by driving. Senate police officers walked alongside him on the four-and-a-half-mile trek. Many of the officers who volunteered for that shift were devout Christians, some of them serious Bible students. They understood how important walking those miles was to Joe and that if he had simply gotten into a car for the sake of convenience, he couldn't have cast his legislative vote in good conscience. That was a wonderful experience—men of different faiths and backgrounds walking side by side in service of what they know is right.

Joe made that long walk over forty times during the twenty-four years he served as a senator. One Friday evening, I was waiting on Joe for dinner with a houseful of distinguished guests. Outside was like a swamp—hot and sticky. I think everyone assumed Joe would take a car back home from work. They were so surprised to see him walk in soaking with sweat. He simply wiped his face off, washed and dried his hands, and sat down at the table. I wasn't surprised. Quite the contrary: that's exactly what I expected of him. Our values did not change when we came to Washington. Instead, they were inevitably put on display. Some people may have viewed us as political oddballs. Nonetheless, our beliefs and practices made us stronger and more committed to our vision of what we could do to help our country.

Once we even had Shabbat in his office in the Hart Building. It was going to be a busy weekend of voting on the Hill, and making the trek back and forth to our Georgetown apartment would have been difficult for us, so we got a room at a hotel near the Senate and planned to have our Shabbat meal in his office. We covered his desk with a white cloth and set our makeshift table complete with candlesticks, challah, wine, and food. Various Senate colleagues, curious to see the rituals of Shabbat, joined us. When it was time for a vote, Joe walked through the tunnel to cast his ballot instead of taking the train from the Hart Building to the Senate chambers, then back to his office to finish the meal. I guess there's a first time for everything.

Then there was the time the Senate chaplain asked Joe if he and I might cohost a Passover seder for the senators. I recall sitting next to Senators Jesse Helms and Paul Wellstone and answering their many questions about the rituals involved in this special meal.

There are some things in public service for which nothing can prepare you. Death threats to your family are one of those things. We received our first one in 1991, just after the Gulf War had ended. Joe had supported the war, and apparently someone took great offense at that. For the next several weeks, we were under twenty-four-hour police protection. Every time I looked outside my kitchen or living room windows, I'd see the agents in dark suits scanning the property. After a while I got used to it, but it never felt normal. It was even more invasive for Joe: agents had to travel with him everywhere he went for his protection.

These things do not go unnoticed by your children. When you enter the public sphere, they become part of it as well. Their relationship to the world changes, and they lose some part of their innocence. Having parents like us, who were on television and in the newspapers, was a challenge for our children to contend with. They succeeded in part because our family unit was so strong. There was "out there," and then there was the reality of our home life. It was important to keep them separate, and especially to keep home life normal, since the other was never going to be. I cherished the simple things, like enjoying a night at home or listening to music with the kids while cooking dinner.

Perhaps one of the greatest challenges was to find time—quality time when we were not exhausted or between chores or people or events—that allowed us to think or read or rest. Working in DC seems glamorous—and at times it most definitely is exciting and a name dropper's paradise. Among the many memorable events that I had occasion to attend was the luncheon given for Leah Rabin at the Israeli ambassador's residence in September 1993 when the Oslo Peace Process was formally launched with the signing of the Oslo Accords at the White House. It was a thrill to sit at the table with others who were also optimistic that this would be a "magical turning moment" in the negotiations between the Israelis and the Palestinians.

I also enjoyed the weekly Ladies of the Senate luncheons. Once I acted as cohost when we honored First Lady Barbara Bush when she was still residing in the White House. I recall her looking out the window, pointing out a colleague who was no longer in the Senate, and commenting on how well he looked. We both laughed. Later, we changed the name of the gathering from Ladies of the Senate to Spouses of the Senate to reflect the increasing number of women senators. And in time, the Take Your Daughters to Work Day became more meaningful as more female senators welcomed the young women into the Senate to discuss their jobs.

I also appreciated the more family-oriented events, like the annual ice cream parties, which assured that all the children of senators and members of Congress would be treated by a group of ice cream manufacturers. Hani loved that party and brought a few neighbor friends every year.

Despite these highlights, the truth is that it was hard to have a normal life, such as inviting friends over for a midweek meal or an impromptu lunch date, because the schedule of a senator can be so unpredictable, the pace relentless and exhausting. Here's an example:

June 1991, spent the weekend in Colorado [where Joe was attending a conference]; on Sunday flew back to Andrews Air Force Base and then driven to Washington National Airport. Missed the 4:30 flight to LaGuardia so we caught the 5 pm flight. From LaGuardia, driven to a black-tie event in Westport. At 9:30 pm we were taken to New Haven, along with Hani and our au pair, to sleep at home. Heavenly. Spent the next day getting the Connecticut house in order and then made a shiva call for a friend's mother before attending a 6:00 pm fundraiser in New York City. [In Judaism, shiva is the week of mourning that follows the burial of a close relative.] Returned to New Haven that night. Left at 7:00 am the next morning, along with child and au pair, for a 9:00 am flight from LaGuardia to D.C. Missed that flight so we took the 9:30 am instead, which left at 9:45. Joe was off to the Senate while I drove the three of us to our Georgetown house. Got myself organized, changed and then off to work after dropping off Hani and au pair at the library.

See what I mean?

My father ran for office the first time when I was one, so it's been a part of my whole life. I have had an amazing privilege and opportunity. I think I have a really positive view of what the government can do and what public service is about, beyond all the cynicism about corruption. I believe in the system and the good of the people who seek to get involved in it. I think it gave me a sense of representing not just myself but my family as well. I knew I would be looked at as being a reflection of my father. In some cases, I think it saved me from some rather disastrous behavior. Being in the public eye taught me responsibility to myself and to others.

BECCA LIEBERMAN

Although my relationship to Joe and his political career was an important part of my identity, over the years I continued to work, choosing employment that satisfied my own independent ways of being a professional and being of service. As any mother who works outside the home can attest, juggling the responsibilities of marriage and motherhood with those of a job can be a high-wire act. Achieving balance can be tricky; one is always in danger of falling. Sometimes the home life takes precedence, and other times it's the job. But there is no other choice: you can't be in two places at once.

When we moved to Washington, I began to build up my career

there. Some people think government officials earn a lot more than they really do. When you are in Congress, in fact, it's a big drain on your finances because you have to maintain two homes: a residence in your home state, which for us was the house in New Haven, and an apartment or house in DC.

My first job in DC was as a senior program officer for the Corporate Council for Mathematics and Science of the National Research Council, a nongovernmental organization, where my focus was on educating people about the importance of technological literacy in schools, work, and the home. Then I worked as a senior associate at APCO Associates, a public affairs company. Headquartered in DC, APCO was founded in 1984 by my friend Margery Kraus.

At APCO, among other things, I developed a series of conferences on health-related issues, from biomedical research and cancer to chronic children's illnesses. I also created a series of seminars for Washington's official international community. These sessions, held in conjunction with the State Department, introduced ambassadors and especially their spouses to how Washington operates—everything from understanding the inner workings of the executive and legislatives branches to following proper protocol and dealing with the media.

One of Joe's opponents later falsely described me as being a lobbyist at APCO. That was not even vaguely true: I was never a lobbyist anywhere and was personally offended by this unwarranted false charge. But when you are in public life or close to someone who is, you need a thick skin. I tried to ignore the attacks, which were indirectly attacks on Joe; they were trying to question my integrity so it would reflect badly on him.

I was finally able to get past the confusion and anger, but as we all know, whatever is put out on the Internet never disappears. All those claims against me as a lobbyist, an "influence peddler," or whatever else some people chose to call me are still floating around. Another curious bit of misinformation on the Internet involves my

FIGURE 1 Ella Wieder in her concentration camp dress. From the Rabbi Samuel and Ella Freilich papers at the United States Holocaust Memorial Museum, Washington, DC.

FIGURE 2 After the war, recovering at a sanatorium. My mother is seated in the first row, second from the right. From the Rabbi Samuel and Ella Freilich papers at the United States Holocaust Memorial Museum, Washington, DC.

FIGURE 5 One of my first baby pictures. From the Rabbi Samuel and Ella Freilich papers at the United States Holocaust Memorial Museum, Washington, DC.

FIGURE 6 My mother, pushing my pram in Prague. From the Rabbi
Samuel and Ella Freilich papers at the United States Holocaust
Memorial Museum, Washington, DC.

FIGURE 7 My parents' joint passport. From the Rabbi Samuel and Ella Freilich papers at the United States Holocaust Memorial Museum, Washington, DC.

AMERICAN JOINT DISTRIBUTION COMMITTEE
PRAHA V, JOSEFOVSKÁ 7.

January 24th, 1949.

United Service for New Americans, Inc.
15 Park Row,   Re: Freilich, Samuel
New York 7, New York.   wife Ella, child
                                                     Hadassa
Gentlemen: USNA #J-3231

May we request your assistance for Dr. Samuel Freilich, who sailed
to the United States on January 4th, 1949.

Dr. Freilich has worked closely with AJDC since liberation, as a
member of the Optant's Bureau in Prague. The Optant's Bureau was
established to assist Jews from the Subcarpathian region, who found
themselves in the Czechlands without citizenship. As an attorney,
Dr. Freilich was able to be of invaluable assistance to them in opt-
ing and securing their citizenship. This was a matter of extreme
importance for the group concerned. At the same time, Dr. Freilich
functioned as a Rabbi and a Hebrew Teacher.

At all times, Dr. Freilich was cooperative and friendly in his
attitude. He was of real assistance to the many thousands of Jews
who required help during the difficult period following liberation.

May we request that you do all in your power to help him in his re-
settlement plans.

Thank you for your kind cooperation.

Sincerely yours,

Helen Kohn
Emigration Director
AJDC Czechoslovakia.

HK:FC
USNA

FIGURE 8 Letter from the American Joint Distribution Committee. From the Rabbi Samuel and Ella Freilich papers at the United States Holocaust Memorial Museum, Washington, D.C.

FIGURE 9 AND 10

At home in Gardner, Massachusetts, with my family: my parents, Rabbi Samuel and Ella Freilich; my brother, Ary; and me. Family photographs from the author's files.

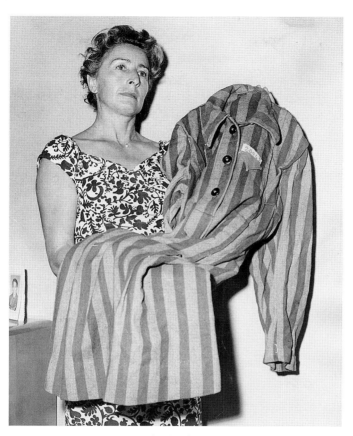

FIGURE 11 My mother holding her concentration
camp uniform. Family photograph from the author's files.

FIGURE 12
My graduation photo.
Family photograph from
the author's files.

FIGURE 13   Our wedding, 1983. Family photograph from the author's files.

FIGURE 14 Joe's first swearing in as senator, 1989. With Vice President George H. W. Bush; our daughter Hani; and my mother-in-law, Marcia Lieberman. Photo courtesy of U.S. Senate Photo.

FIGURE 15 A photo shoot at our home in New Haven. Our daughter Hani is on Joe's lap. Behind him, from left, are our children Becca, Matt, and Ethan. Family photograph from the author's files.

FIGURE 16 With my mother-in-law, Marcia Lieberman, and
our daughter Hani at a Senate event in
Washington, DC. Photo courtesy of U.S. Senate Photo.

FIGURE 17 Celebrating a Senate reelection victory at our house in New Haven
with my mother-in-law, Marcia Lieberman, on the far left, and my mother,
Ella Freilich, on the right. Family photograph from the author's files.

FIGURE 18 Toasting Leah Rabin and the Oslo Peace Process, 1993.
Courtesy of the Embassy of Israel to the United States.

FIGURE 19 At a Senate celebration in Washington.
My mother was so excited to meet President Bill Clinton.
Official White House Photograph.

FIGURE 20 A luncheon celebration with First Lady Hillary Clinton
and Second Lady Tipper Gore. Photo courtesy
of the U.S. Senate Photo.

FIGURE 21 Who would have thought that my unusual and consistently mispronounced name would become part of the 2000 Democratic National Convention? Family photograph from the author's files.

FIGURE 22 At a special Senate luncheon in honor of First Lady Michelle Obama and Second Lady Jill Biden. Photo courtesy of the U.S. Senate Photo.

FIGURE 23 Passover 2017 in Kfar Blum, Israel, with our grandchildren.
Three years later our 12th grandchild was born. Photo by Alexander Seleznyov.

birth. I was born in a Prague hospital in 1948, but some news reports claimed that I was born in a Czech refugee camp for Holocaust survivors. Go figure.

I remained at APCO from 1993 to 1997 when so much was going on that needed my attention. I had a busy life as a senator's wife, and there were the needs of our family, as well as the demands of running two homes. I decided to give myself a little more flexibility by forming my own company, HFL Associates, which I ran for a few years. My focus was on nonprofit organizations, especially those working with children and adults with disabilities, including the Special Olympics. Another client was the American Committee for Shaare Zedek Medical Center, a multicultural hospital in Jerusalem. Our emphasis was on women's health issues. A major program I launched, Sister to Sister, connected women of different nationalities with common health concerns. I also initiated and organized an Everyone Has a Heart campaign to link American and Israeli women and generate awareness of coronary heart disease in women.

These assignments were especially satisfying even if my life remained a multitasker's challenge. There were the responsibilities to my work and ensuring that my business interests didn't conflict with my husband's job. There were the usual concerns of a working parent—an absent sitter, a child with strep throat. And then there was public life. Anytime I went out, I had to look presentable and speak carefully so as not to contradict or embarrass Joe. When we traveled, whether domestically or internationally, we were mindful that we were not private citizens but representatives of our country and needed to act accordingly. Sometimes we opted to stay home rather than go out for dinner because we were tired and didn't know how much of the meal would be taken up talking to the people who approached us. I'll never forget the time we took some of the family to Madison, Connecticut, for a much-needed vacation. There we were on the beach, not being able to walk more than two feet without being grilled about what was going on in DC at that moment.

Of course, Joe owed it to his constituents to hear them out, but that didn't mean it was easy on the family or him. I am not complaining; we understood that this was all part of the job.

Another concern of mine during this time was my aging parents. My mother was holding her own, but my father's Parkinson's disease progressed to the point where he needed more care than she could provide at home. She would find him running down the hallway of their apartment building, screaming that he was being chased by the Nazis. Eventually we moved him to the Hebrew Home for the Aged in Riverdale. At this point, he could no longer speak or walk, so his wheelchair had a number on it as a way to identify him. All of a sudden, my father, who had outmaneuvered the Nazis and made a new life for himself in America, was identified by a number. This pained me greatly, but the sting was lessened when I'd push him in his wheelchair while his grandchildren scampered about. My mother visited every day except Shabbat and made sure he was dressed as always in a crisp shirt, tie, and jacket. It was painful to witness his decline, though I recognize it is an inevitable part of the life cycle. Sometimes when I visited prior to Shabbat, I would sing his favorite *Shabbes* tunes, and he joined in as best he could, warming my heart. I remain thankful that we were able to keep him comfortable until the very end. He passed away in 1993.

SEVEN

A Stone from Auschwitz

By nature we are like all other human beings,
yet our people is unlike others, because our life is different,
our history is different, our teacher is the Exile.

I. L. Peretz | Yiddish writer and playwright from Poland

I was at work at APCO on a Thursday morning in January 1995 when I got a call from the Clinton White House. Would I join the American delegation to the fiftieth anniversary of the liberation of Auschwitz? The invitation took my breath away, and in a cracked voice I responded, "If I can go . . . I *have* to go." My first fleeting thoughts were of my schedule, job, six-year-old daughter Hani, and Joe. The delegation was leaving shortly, so there was not much time to prepare for what might be the most important journey of my life.

I had not been thinking about this upcoming anniversary. I don't spend my life contemplating such milestones, despite (or maybe because of) the fact I am the daughter of survivors. I had never been to any of the camps and had not planned to go. I did visit Czechoslovakia because I wanted to see where my family had lived and where I was born. I did not have a desire to go to the places where my family was sent to die.

The invitation took me by surprise. The mundane logistical problems associated with a major trip mixed with the painful memories, making it difficult to decide whether to go. I called my mother, and she was very apprehensive. She feared for my safety. Who would go with me? Who would I stand with at the ceremony? Why is it necessary for me to go?

But in the end, I concluded that *she* was why it was necessary for me to go—she and my father and their relatives and friends. I had to go.

This recounting of my experiences was printed in the *Congressional Record* on August 9, 1995.

TUESDAY, JANUARY 24 . . . IN-FLIGHT TO FRANKFURT

The last few days, the only preparation time I have, I cry often. I call Auschwitz survivors, friends of my mother, for words of support. For the most part, they remain quiet, saying simply, "Go in peace. Bring back peace."

I am on a Delta flight and I've just finished reading some articles from the US Holocaust Memorial in Washington—excruciating material—describing concentration camps in the vicinity of Auschwitz and Birkenau. I wipe the tears from my eyes, transfixed by this world of cruelty and torture, realizing I am soon to visit this symbol of all evil.

The descriptions of the concentration camps are incomprehensible—another world, another place. The screen above me plays out O. J. Simpson's trial, Japan's earthquake. I watch the survivors in Japan and wonder, *How can you not feel for these people?* How can you not feel for their homelessness, their cold, their devastation . . . and I can't understand what happened in the concentration camps.

I find myself looking at a picture of Joe in the *Washington Post* . . . sweet darling . . . The picture made me feel stronger. Now Newt Gingrich is on the screen. And Chris Dodd. The world intrudes.

Before I left, my mother asked me to bring back dirt from Auschwitz. Nearly all of her family was burned and pulverized into that dirt, that stinking evil earth . . . do you bring it home? Is this their

grave, entire families? Where are they buried? The ovens? The crematoria? The pits? Fifty years later the stench and screams will not
be there.

How evil can people be? Watch the news and you see in snippets:
Chechnya, Bosnia, the Middle East. But the sheer enormity of this
evil that I am traveling to witness is incomprehensible. The enormity
and the organization of it all. I know there are criminals who do
ugly, horrible things every day. But the Holocaust was the product
of a whole criminal society, a society of people who were educated,
literate, loved music, loved art, loved literature. And look what they
did with such efficiency, with so little evidence of guilt.

WEDNESDAY, JANUARY 25 . . .

FRANKFURT, GERMANY, AND WARSAW, POLAND

A three-hour layover in the morning in Frankfurt at the new, empty
airport. So antiseptic it is scary to me, somehow. All the signs are in
German. It is my first time in Germany, and I'm feeling guarded.
I speak mostly with a woman from the State Department, telling
her about my background, my mother. I pick up the newspaper, the
Frankfurter Allgemeine Zeitung, and there is a picture of Hitler! It
was taken in 1944, and he looked tired, old. It shows him viewing
something with a magnifying glass. He knew then his war was fail-
ing. But he pushed on with the Final Solution, as furiously as ever.
It was in 1944 that my mother was herded to the camps. Even as the
war effort was faltering, the Nazis pressed on to kill the Jews.

In the afternoon, we fly to Warsaw and are picked up by embassy people and brought to the Marriott hotel, where delegates
from around the world are arriving. That evening, I go to a reception
at the residence of the U.S. Ambassador to Poland, Nicholas Rey,
along with some of the other members of our delegation, including
Miles Lerman of the United States Holocaust Memorial Council and his wife, Chris, an Auschwitz survivor; Ambassador John

Kordek, now with DePaul University; and Jan Nowak, director of the Polish American Congress. The head of our delegation, Nobel Peace Prize winner Elie Wiesel, and the Clinton administration's Assistant Secretary of State, Richard Holbrooke, will join us the next day.

We begin to talk about the controversy surrounding the ceremony planned for Friday. Auschwitz was initially intended for Polish political prisoners; Poles look at Auschwitz as a national shrine and museum. It seems as though they wanted the commemoration to be more of a generic event, with no special emphasis on Jewish deaths. No praying of the *Kaddish* [the thirteenth-century prayer said by mourners that extols G-d's greatness, even as their faith is being tested by their loss]. In response, some are planning an alternative service on Thursday at Birkenau. Preposterous, but true, Elie's words, "Not all victims were Jews, but all Jews were victims," need to be repeated over and over again.

I am concerned about the controversy but, at the same time, I do not want to lose sight of the larger reason for our being there. I am moved to say to everyone there that I understand there's controversy around us. But we should not forget how incredible it is that we're all here together, from all over the world, to commemorate something that happened 50 years ago that, at the time, nobody wanted to hear about. We need to talk about the details, but we should not lose sight of the fact that we're here as representatives of our country, bearing witness to what happened to so many people.

We decide that those of us who wanted to go to the alternative service will meet the next morning in a hotel lobby. I have mixed feelings. As a Jew and the daughter of survivors, I want to go to Birkenau. As a member of the official American delegation, I am worried that it might detract from protocol if I deviate from the schedule, which includes a ceremony at Jagiellonian University in Krakow. But everyone assures me that the American delegation will be sufficiently represented at the university.

We arrive in Krakow, a city left untouched by bombing. Some say it is a "small Prague." Over 25% of its population was Jewish and 90% of its Jews were annihilated. Now tours are advertised to show where Spielberg filmed "Schindler's List" in the Jewish "ghetto" area. The Ariel Cafe is booming with Eastern European/Jewish foods and Yiddish music. The synagogue is old—dating back to the 1400s. Stone markers from Jewish cemeteries are preserved as part of the wall.

I check into the Forum Hotel in the city. Leaders from all over the world are arriving . . . Ambassadors, Presidents. Kings, Prime Ministers. Security measures are being put into place. Metal detectors assembled. Dogs brought in. I find real irony in the contrast; here it is, fifty years later, and all the forces of authority are being marshaled for our protection, whereas before they would have come to sweep many of us up.

All the security precautions also remind me of my mother's concerns for my safety. I don't personally feel threatened, but I begin to realize what she was talking about. I understand we have to be careful, and I know what she felt about my coming here, and how horrible it would be if something happens to me where so much had happened to her. A double-suicide bombing in Israel occurred just days before, reminding us that, for Jews, the world can still be a very dangerous place.

News of the alternative ceremony has been spreading by word-of-mouth, and interest in it grows. Originally planned by Jewish organizations and Israelis, it takes on a life of its own, and suddenly includes everyone—not only the American Ambassador and other delegates from the American group, but every delegation from around the world decides to send representatives.

And so I go to the camps, 50 years after my mother left.

Back then, no one "knew" what was going on there. No brave partisans bombed the tracks and rescued the inmates. No one seemed to care or reach out. And now, all the nations of the world are represented as the buses go to Birkenau. We travel with the Israeli delegation in front of us, escorted by heavy security. Elie Wiesel, Ambassador and Mrs. Rey, Jan Nowak (who tells me he will go because as a Pole and a Catholic, he must; he was one of the first to alert British leaders to the tragedy of the Holocaust).

Our bus pulls into a large parking area and we exit along with hundreds and hundreds of people. I walk with Elie Wiesel, the Ambassador and his wife, and the others over the rocky, muddy ground. I am arm in arm with Sigmund Strochlitz of Birkenau and Connecticut, a friend of Elie and Joe. He reminds me a little bit of my father.

Where are we? I look around and there are mobs of people around us walking in silence. We were warned about the coldness at the camps. But the weather is warm in Krakow . . . until we walk farther into the camps and then the coldness begins to set in—a different kind of coldness, eerie . . . heavy. Suddenly I realize we are walking near railroad tracks, and Sigmund begins to speak: "This was where the train ran into the camp. The train was able to take people straight to the end—to the crematoria." This is Birkenau, a death camp. An enormously vast space that was devoted to murder.

I thought again of what my mother had told me, vague references to gassings, chimneys, SS, kapos [prisoners forced to act as overseers or functionaries for the SS in concentration camps]. She always said it was a shock when the Nazis took over, since her family had lived through the First World War and "it wasn't so bad." Yet her entire family had been exterminated. She remembers the screams when they were sent to a shower that they thought would be gas and there was a "mistake," and they remained alive. She remembers the piles of bodies left in their clothes, a kapo's beating, sleeping stuffed in the wooden bunks, alternating heads and feet to make more room.

She remembers falling deathly ill from eating soup that had human bones in the bowl.

For my mother, Auschwitz was not a final destination. She was sent to the Wehrmacht Fabrik company near Stuttgart, where she worked as a slave laborer at night and slept during the day. A Nazi official assigned her to an office to work with other women who knew different languages. Eventually she was liberated from a subcamp of Dachau and took a train to Prague. In the days following her return, she and hundreds of others would run to the station whenever a new train pulled in, desperately searching for family, friends, familiar faces. And they were never there. And then she stopped running. For two years or more, she would go to the basement and cry until she couldn't cry anymore.

I knew all of this—the nightmares; the casual references like, "They all died"; the guilt in remaining a survivor; the questions. I think again of the soil she wanted me to bring back. "They have no graves," she told me. "It would have been better if the mothers were separated from the children, so they didn't have to see them murdered in front of their eyes." So, I should have been prepared, no? I should have been ready. Although we never talked in detail about the camps, I was totally aware. I always knew about her background. I bear some of the hidden scars of a survivor's child—it doesn't take much for my thoughts to go to a dark place. And so, why was I shocked? Why is the walk into Birkenau so terrifying? Let me take you with me.

First, we crowd together as delegates for the most part, others from the survivors' community. I notice a group with a banner that seemed odd. I ask Sigmund and he tells me that this is the banner of "Mengele's children," the survivors of Mengele's experiments—his "children" and "children's children." Then Sigmund shows me where Mengele had stood to make his selection. He shows me the women's and men's barracks. We keep walking forward. I am in awe of what my parents lived through.

I have arrived at a different planet. This is not the moon. The moon has been explored. This is a distant planet and most who journeyed there are now ashes near the crematoria. The others had to repress, to black out, to forget, in order to go on. This planet is one of surrealistic impressions. The smokestacks. The endless fields with numbered barracks. The latrine house with round holes for toilets in two rows, each nearly touching the other but with enough space for a sadistic kapo to walk down the middle and whip the women who took too long to defecate. The bunks with beds . . . eight or nine in each small slab. No matter how much you read about the place, when you see it with your own eyes, it takes on another dimension. The Jews were looked at like animals. Actually, like less than animals. The Nazis treated their dogs better than us. And we continue to walk.

I feel the people around me, walking down this frightful road. The American Ambassador to Poland had chosen to walk with us for this "unofficial" event. The American in me, yearning to believe and hope that the world will stand united against cruelty of this proportion. The Jew in me, fearful of the repetitions of history . . . the Israeli flag . . . a refuge . . . a homeland . . . The wife of a United States senator, proud to be part of the American delegation, led by Elie Wiesel, bearing witness to history.

We continue our walk until we arrive at the crematoria. What can I say? I hold Sigmund's arm tightly. What can I say? I came unequipped to the planet of death, of torture, of "endless nights," as our delegation leader describes it. Everything in front of me told me I could never believe anything after this place.

All of these people around me walk with us in silence. The program takes place, people speak, people shout. *Kaddish* is said and we think perhaps it would have been better to keep our silence—just *Kaddish* and no words. But then we sing "Hatikvah" [Israel's national anthem] and march back to the buses.

Auschwitz is next. A tour of one hour. I find a stone for Dad's grave. I decide not to bring the soil back with me. I had brought a plastic bag, thinking I might. But I decide no. I will not bring soil from the planet of death. Several people tell me about the bones found in the soil 50 years later, some of them the bones of babies. If one is a believer, then the souls have ascended to heaven and what is left should be left behind in peace on Earth. These people, the unsuspecting, the victims, the *K'doshim* [the holy ones] were not left behind in peace. I will not take their soil. I don't want any part of that soil.

Yet a rock endures from the beginning. It waits silently, protectively, coldly. The rock was there before and the rock is there after, and the rock bears witness. This egg-shaped rock will go on my father's grave. *It is small, Daddy, but it is tough, like you. It survives. And remember, in your memoirs, when you asked, "Who should say the mourner's Kaddish?" Daddy, we said Kaddish as we stood at Birkenau. Our voices, the young, the old, the victims, the onlookers stood together.*

Elie Wiesel's friend, Pierre, of France, goes with me to Auschwitz. A large, burly man, somewhat irreverent, quite cynical and sarcastic, takes me to his father's place at Auschwitz. Block 11. The death bunker was the destination of his father who knew 12 languages and served as *schreiber* [writer] for the place. When his Hungarian father was in Auschwitz, a beautiful young woman was brought in and he helped her. Somehow, they managed to fall in love and as she left, she told him where she was from in Paris and that she would meet him there after the war. When he survived, he went to the address. They met and married.

Short stories, sweet, bitter, unreal. We are shown an enormous room filled with suitcases that are all labeled with the names of the people to whom they once belonged. We see piles of hair. Eyeglasses. Wooden legs. Prayer shawls. It reminds me of the United States Holocaust Memorial Museum in Washington, where similar exhibits exist. I would wonder from time to time why Washington should be the site for such a museum. What is appropriate about the nation's capital? Here in Auschwitz, I see the answer. I understand the importance of keeping evidence of the evil on display, and I also understand that there is a better chance of such a museum remaining open in Washington than in almost any other place. Who knows what will happen here at Auschwitz in years to come? We already know how the Communists kept a lid on the enormity of crimes against the Jews. We do not know what the future will hold, and so it is right for us to have a museum of the Holocaust at the center of the world's oldest, greatest, strongest democracy.

Thursday night, we are taken to a concert at the Slowacki Theatre in Krakow, where we hear an orchestral piece written by a Pole for the occasion. It is so jagged and jarring—deliberately created so, because it was about the camps—that I want to get out of there. I had gotten through the day and I want to run. It is so stifling. Finally it is over, and we think, *oh G-d. Let's just sit down and have some life*, so we go to the Ariel Cafe. Let me sit here and be a part of life again. Elie Wiesel is there, and I recall how often in his book, *Night*, he talks about the darkness, and we're in the land of night and we have to keep a certain part of ourselves in the night so that we don't lose it. Elie writes from that darkness, yet wants us to hope for the future. Surrounded by the light and life and sights and sounds of the Ariel Cafe, I want to be lively and have hope, but it is too hard.

FRIDAY, JANUARY 27 . . . AUSCHWITZ

On Friday we take buses that go directly to the crematoria area at Auschwitz. I see Václav Havel on my bus. When we arrive, there are so many people packed together and walking forward that it is hard to stand without being pushed. I think to myself, irreverently, that after 50 years, people are pushing to get to the front of the line. I think, too, that we could have been those people 50 years ago, told to undress, having our hair cut. It was people like us who walked into this camp.

I see all the world's media gathered together, pushing for position, for the best views, wanting to hear every word, and I think, *Where were you 50 years ago when you were truly needed?* If they had video cameras then, if people actually knew what was going on, would it have made a difference? So many of us have witnessed destruction and violence. Sometimes the visuals make a difference and sometimes they don't.

After a few minutes, the crowd settles in. I stand near Richard Holbrooke and Jan Nowak [a Polish journalist and writer who was part of the Resistance during World War II]. The program features representatives from many delegations and religions, including our own delegation leader, Elie Wiesel. I am moved when I hear the ceremony begin—after all—with the *Kaddish* and another Hebrew prayer for the dead, *El Maleh*. It is a change resulting from a meeting Elie had with Polish President Lech Walesa the day before, as was a reference to Jewish deaths in Walesa's speech.

The formal tribute begins in the growing cold air. A poignant moment occurs when the Boy Scouts and Girl Scouts of Poland walk around to give out hot coffee. The elderly, in particular, reach out for the cups. Watching these children acting so charitably 50 years after the Holocaust somehow gives us a warm feeling about the present and the future, even as it conjures up memories of all the other children, in different kinds of uniforms, who died at this place. There was the story of the little boy who jumped off a train bound for a concentration camp with an apple in his hand. The train was at a station, and the SS caught him, took him by his legs and bashed him against the train until he was dead. A few minutes later, one of the murderers was casually eating the apple. And there was the story my father told me of the parents who tossed their babies from the trains into the arms of strangers along the side of the tracks, hoping against hope that those families would make a new home for their children.

Tears come to my eyes as I contrast the moments. An international display of solidarity, tribute, apology. Late, painful and yet a moment of hope. Then, it is over, and together we walk in the mud to our buses, past those in prison uniforms (Are these actors? Family members of survivors?), national costumes and, mostly, plain street clothes. Everyone's shoes and boots are covered with mud.

FRIDAY NIGHT AND SATURDAY, JANUARY 27 AND 28 . . .
SHABBAT . . . KRAKOW

When I learned before the trip that I had to remain in Poland for Shabbat, alone and far from my family and synagogue, I worried about what I would do. But I am not alone and, as it turns out, staying in Krakow becomes one of the most special Shabbats I have ever experienced. After the marches, the ceremonies, the journey to the other planet, to stop for Shabbat and to share the special moment with people from all over the world is meaningful. We sit together on Friday night with the chief rabbis of England, Poland, Ukraine, Italy, and Jews from England, Germany, Krakow, Warsaw, Israel, America. Rabbi Avi Weiss of Riverdale, New York, is with us. He is the activist who protested the original plans for the ceremony and who has become so much of a celebrity that when the police arrested him in Poland for tearing down a sign that said, "Protect the cross against Jews and Masons," they asked to take his picture and have his autograph.

We all sing and pray together and tell stories. Of particular poignancy are the stories of the young Eastern European Jews. Since the fall of Communism, they are learning of their Jewishness. Their family trees were deeply fractured by the Holocaust; many have no grandparents. Some were born to parents who were hidden with Polish Catholic families when their parents were sent to their deaths.

One young man learned just three years ago that he was Jewish. Perhaps some of them are descended from the babies tossed from the death trains. How ironic that Hitler's criteria for determining who was Jewish—in some instances, the association was quite remote—are the same for many of these individuals who have now embraced their Judaism.

The next day, on our way to services, I walk behind Rabbi Weiss and see him with his prayer shawl over his jacket. People along the way, not accustomed to seeing Jews, stop and stare. Some take pictures. And I think, *Is it gaudy, is it showy, is it obnoxious for our group to be so obvious in such a place?* That is my first reaction, but then I remember Auschwitz and the displayed prayer shawls taken from the Jews who were annihilated, and how the descendants were alive and walking to the synagogue, and it seems right that Rabbi Weiss is wearing his prayer shawl.

Our Shabbat services are, strangely enough, joyous. We are all happy to be together, to be alive. We feel the history of the tragedy in our depths. We share our common history, common pain. We all have questions and no real answers. As we call out in our prayers, rising above and beyond the evil planet of Auschwitz and Birkenau, the planet that bore witness to our people's destruction, we all turn to the very G-d that had not answered the prayers of our parents and their parents as the crematoria burnt their bodies into ashes.

Nothing on that planet gives you faith. Nothing there gives you hope for mankind. And yet, as I walked with my fellow travelers that day, as I felt their bodies near me, heard their feet in the mud and stones, walking silently, I knew our walk was prayer. Our walk might defy—bear witness. Our walk might challenge any evils as great, as powerful, as wicked, and so as we prayed, we all felt history around us. We were defying Hitler and his henchmen. We were rising above the defiled and tortured and abandoned. We were free Jews singing to G-d, responsible for one another.

Am yisrael chai. "The people of Israel live." The Israeli flag was around us, and we knew how great was our need for a place of refuge, wanting to trust, but learning the bitter lessons of history. We Americans felt how special our country is, a country where a Jew could become a senator, and where his wife, the daughter of survivors, could be chosen by the President to participate in the commemoration of the liberation—the destruction—of the planet of death.

I had to go. No matter how much you read, and how much you hear about it and how much you talk to your family—even if you are as close to the Holocaust as the child of survivors—you have to go there and see this horrendously evil, evil, evil place that stinks in its profanity, that is so ugly that it shakes your belief in everything, your belief in mankind and your faith in G-d. And you won't understand. But you will know.

Once back home with my family, I was anxious for the day when I could travel to my father's grave in New Jersey and place the stone from Auschwitz on the ground that contains his earthly remains, confident that his spirit survives in eternity, never again to live on a planet of death. Never again.

EIGHT

Election 2000

*There are only two ways to live your life. One is as though nothing
is a miracle. The other is as though everything is a miracle.*

Albert Einstein

The events surrounding the 2000 presidential election have been
dissected, analyzed, and discussed in countless articles and books,
including the one I authored with Joe, *An Amazing Adventure*. I
don't see the value of rehashing old news, but even with the passage
of time, certain moments from the campaign have stayed with me.

One such moment was the day in August 2000 when Vice President Al Gore publicly announced that he had chosen my husband
as his running mate. The night before, at dinner with the Gores,
I spontaneously raised my glass in thanks to Al—speaking as the
daughter of survivors—for choosing Joe as his running mate. Gore
said he wanted me to talk about my background in my introductory
remarks, since my story seemed to embody the American dream.

The official announcement took place at the War Memorial
Plaza in Gore's hometown of Nashville, Tennessee. A crowd of over
ten thousand had braved the blistering summer sun to participate in
this pivotal moment in American democracy. My family was there,
somewhere in the back of that mass of people. As the temperature
climbed north of 100 degrees and the humidity was even worse, Al
and Joe stripped off their suit jackets and rolled up their shirtsleeves.

An equally sweat-drenched church choir sang "G-d Bless America." I thought it was marvelous that a Christian chorus was welcoming the first Jewish vice-presidential candidate onto the national stage.

I'd spoken publicly about being the daughter of survivors as well as an immigrant, but never in front of such a large crowd. Somehow, looking out at the cheering, hope-filled faces gave me new courage. In one incredible instant, I saw the connection—with a clarity that had previously eluded me—between my family's past, the present, and the future of my family and country. Here I was, the child of survivors, a proud Jew, an immigrant, and the wife of this man I dearly loved, now being nominated for national office. The speechwriters and campaign staff had written carefully planned remarks that hit all the political talking points. However, that day their note cards felt stiff and irrelevant in comparison to what was in my heart. I wasn't only speaking on behalf of Joe and myself. This historic moment was beyond both of us. I was here to represent immigrants like me who had prospered, thanks to the opportunities America had given them. I was also impelled to give voice to those who had not been so lucky: the victims of the Holocaust. In Hebrew, we call them *neshamas*—souls. I sensed their presence as I approached the podium to speak. Surprisingly, I felt calm and self-assured. It wasn't me speaking, really; I was just the conduit.

When the master of ceremonies introduced me, he mispronounced my name. I was used to it—people were always mangling my name—and ignored the gaffe as I positioned myself behind the podium. My voice was steady as I spoke to the crowd:

Here I am, speaking from my heart, in this place that commemorates World War II. And here I am, the daughter of survivors from the Holocaust, the most horrendous thing that has happened. And here I am in the place that commemorates the American heroes, the soldiers who actually liberated my mother from Dachau and Auschwitz. And so I stand before you very deeply, sincerely thankful that I am an American, grateful that we have such a wonderful, wonderful family and friends in the Gores, and that they've made this bold, wonderful choice to help us be part of the ticket that's going to win!

Let me end now with just this one statement, and I say this to all of you here and all of you who are watching this on television, and this is real:

Whether you or your family emigrated from Europe, Africa, Mexico, Latin America, or Asia, I am standing here for you! This country is our country! This land is your land, and anything is possible for us!

The sound from the crowd when I finished speaking was like nothing I had ever heard before. As the powerful roar washed over me, I tried to look at the individual faces of the people with whom I had just shared a deep part of my soul. I felt connected to them not just as fellow Americans but as *humans*. Amazingly, impossibly, and so wonderfully, there I was, touching people's hearts on the world stage. When you are an immigrant and the daughter of survivors, the last thing you normally would do is stand before a group of strangers and call attention to your differences; most of us spend a lifetime trying to fit in. But Vice President Gore encouraged me to share my inner thoughts at this historic moment and to highlight those differences. I was standing in front of the world, a witness to survival and the blessings of freedom.

Later, I heard my husband tell the crowd that each time a barrier falls for one person, the doors of opportunity open wider for every other American. My heart swelled when he invoked our G-d of Abraham, and said, "Maker of all miracles, I thank you for bringing me to this extraordinary moment in my life."

Though I knew I had made the right decision to speak from the heart, I didn't understand how deep a nerve I had touched until a week later, when I spoke again, this time at the Democratic National Convention in Los Angeles. As I looked out incredulously at the sea of blue and white signs that bore one word, "Hadassah," and heard thousands of voices chant my name in unison, over and over (this time pronouncing it correctly), I knew I had penetrated some corner of our national consciousness. By raising my own voice, I was giving voice to many others.

This is what I said that memorable August evening:

Wow! It's hard to believe that it was only one week ago that Tipper and I were in my hometown of Gardner, Massachusetts, to celebrate this new and momentous adventure.

To all of our family, our old friends and our new friends: we thank you for your support and your enthusiasm. It has been overwhelming and gratifying. Tonight I want to share with you some personal thoughts about my Joe. What public service means to him, and how his service has been shaped by the values that are his heart and soul.

For Joe, family, faith, neighborhood, congregation, and community are the guideposts of his life, orienting the choices he makes and the causes he champions. Community keeps Joe grounded and reminds him of his commitment to respectful living. It reminds him to embrace our nation's diversity and celebrate our differences. It reminds him of the Republic he serves, one nation, under G-d, indivisible, with liberty and justice for all.

Joe often says that effective public service casts a wide net and gathers the community together to support one another. A kind of approach that demands living up to your obligations, but leaves no person behind. An approach that invites collaboration and rewards the results. Some folks have said my husband is just a "regular Joe." He is that—and more.

His connection to the larger community has molded a vision that is anything but ordinary. When Al Gore chose my husband as his running mate, this country got a man whose mission in life is inspired by the people he serves and the community he loves.

Ladies and gentlemen . . . my husband, my best friend, and the love of my life . . . the next Vice President of the United States of America . . . Joe Lieberman.

> Imagine you're out there on the stage at the convention like I was in 2000 and everyone is watching you. I was only there for a split second, but still, especially at age 12, you have the sense that everyone is watching what you're doing on this public stage. It can be scary. To me though, it was something profound and meaningful that I was glad to be a part of.
>
> HANI LIEBERMAN

Once again, I had spoken from the heart. My experience in Nashville had left me with little patience for canned remarks. Throughout the rest of the campaign, I had staffers in my ear, repeatedly advising me of the importance of being politically correct. "It's important to win people over on these points," they would emphasize before I gave a speech. Sometimes I found their advice unsatisfactory and would simply speak my mind. When you are in the midst of a campaign of this magnitude, you are pulled in too many directions. Speaking candidly was the only way I could stay grounded. I discovered that an honest back-and-forth with people created a strong foundation of mutual trust. The truth is, it's always been my instinct to talk to people directly. I'm so glad that my style seems to work because I can't do it any other way.

> Watching my sister, Hadassah, introduce Joe at the Democratic Convention in the Staples Center was a defining moment for me. She had given many talks and speeches but never anything of this magnitude, with millions watching and listening. I was sitting next to my mother, surrounded by the countless thousands of people waving placards with the name Hadassah and shouting her name. I was nervous for her, terrified that under such pressure, it could go bad and become a massive humiliation for her. Then out she comes, perfectly put together: perfect posture, perfect makeup, perfect hands over the heart, perfect diction, words emoted in a way that to me was Oprah-esque. There wasn't a person who watched it who didn't react with affection and respect for this woman who had risen to this occasion so spectacularly. This was a moment when I realized what my sister was made of.
>
> ARY FREILICH | Hadassah's brother

Throughout the 2000 campaign, immigrants approached me with their own powerful stories. Military veterans, including those who had served in World War II, would come to shake my hand; survivors would push up their shirtsleeves to show the numbers tattooed on their arms. There were so many tears that the Secret Service would joke about how I evoked the waterworks. Later I spoke to Jim Kennedy, Joe's former press secretary, whose father had been a sergeant in the Forty-Second Rainbow Division, one of two Army divisions that liberated the camp at Dachau where my mother was sent after Auschwitz. He told me how moved he had been by my speech in Nashville.

In some ways, being a political spouse is not so different from being a rabbi's daughter. There's the ever-present awareness of being scrutinized, the concern about keeping up appearances, and always, always watching what you say in public. I suppose you could say I received an advanced degree in life in the public eye when Joe was the attorney general of Connecticut and then a senator, but that kind of attention pales in comparison to what happens when your spouse is running for national office.

When Al Gore selected Joe as his running mate, we were at home in Connecticut. After the flurry of calls and the arrival of our team of handlers, we were scheduled to leave for Nashville in the morning, where the official announcement would be made. The media were swarming around our house, and we were all in a daze, but the garbage had to be taken out. I didn't think this basic household chore was such a noteworthy event, but there are photos capturing the fact that I had gone outside—barefoot. Welcome to life in the spotlight.

There was so much to learn. Now that we were operating on a national stage, the Secret Service had to educate us on various security matters. We could no longer lock the doors of our house or hotel room because in the event of an emergency, the agents would need easy access. When exiting a car, we needed to wait for an agent to open the door, indicating that they had secured the area and it was safe to leave the vehicle.

Once I was waiting for Joe at a campaign event in Florida. I was happy to be there but hadn't seen him in several days and missed our time together. I stood on the curb as his car pulled up. When the Secret Service opened the door, Joe continued to talk to a staff member for quite some time while I waited for him to finish the conversation, exit the car, and greet me. Admittedly it was a trivial thing, but I was annoyed. When Joe got out of the car, he looked at me and read my expression, but I knew what I had to do. As he took my arm, we smiled and waved to the row of photographers. The cameras flashed; I looked happy in the photo. In private life, you don't think about every expression on your face and don't try to correct every movement. Yet there is a reason you are willing to accept that level of scrutiny and self-discipline: you believe in something greater than your ego—your devotion to the public service in which your husband and you are engaged.

Perhaps the hardest lesson to internalize about public life is that it occurs simultaneously with your private life. There's a randomness to the schedule of a political campaign that makes things even more difficult. If you are nursing an infant, you do so while campaigning. If there are elderly parents to tend to, bills to pay, a bat mitzvah to plan, you do so while campaigning. A tip I learned from Tipper Gore: schedule in at least a few days at home every week, just to keep your home and family life in order—and your sanity.

For us, certain things were sacrosanct. One was carving out time to visit my mother in Riverdale. At this point, she had lost the ability to speak and was confined to her bed at the Hebrew Home for the Aged. I traveled to see her as much as I could. Often I spent the entire day sitting by her bed while she slept, watching the clock and willing her to wake up before I had to go. Those days were tough. Depending on when she got up, we might have only a few minutes together before I had to leave for whatever event was next on my schedule.

Another thing that was nonnegotiable was Shabbat. Not only did we insist on having our sacred time then, but we also had a block of forty-five minutes prior to sundown built into the schedule each Friday so that we could get cleaned up and changed into proper Shabbat clothing. To us, the Sabbath was just as important as making an extra campaign stop—more important actually. If we didn't stay true to who we were, what was the point of running for office in the first place? Shabbat is a reprieve, a day to cherish. At the time, I told Joe I couldn't imagine how we could live a political life without it. During those incredibly scheduled times, Shabbat became even more restorative for us. And our campaign staff ended up loving the time off on Friday nights and Saturdays.

> The reaction to our religious observance did take some unusual turns. I turned on the TV one night early in the campaign and found Reverend Bob Jones on *Larry King Live,* saying how great it was that I was a person of faith who was willing to talk about it in public.
>
> JOE LIEBERMAN

Some of Joe's advisers had asked him to downplay his religious beliefs, to keep his religiosity "in check" for fear that there would be a backlash of some kind. He was, after all, the first *Jewish* major party candidate in American history. Of course he refused, as did I. I would not keep my prayers quiet. In fact, Joe and I prayed in our house in New Haven the very morning they announced he was chosen to run for vice president. I'll always be proud of him for publicly embracing his relationship to G-d rather than downplaying it due to political pressure.

> You have a sense that everyone is watching what you're doing on this public stage. G-d is also watching, and He has His own ongoing camera. When my father was selected to be the vice-presidential candidate and the media was at our front door, my mother walked out and kissed the mezuzah. It was all over TV. I don't know how many people went to put a mezuzah on their door after that. This was one way in which my parents' religious observance was on display. To me that was very meaningful and profound, and helped me in my own religious observance.
>
> HANI LIEBERMAN

Another item not up for discussion was Hani's schedule, whether it was breakfast, school, or her other activities. Our other children were older—and they were eager to campaign as much as possible—but Hani was only twelve and we didn't want to disrupt her life any more than we had to. She had her own Secret Service detail and transportation.

> I grew up in a unique situation because of my father's job. The Senate schedule is crazy, but not in the way of a doctor, lawyer, or businessman. It's on a national scale. But still I think my parents always made me a priority. For example, my father would always come to different events at my school. He rearranged his schedule a lot for me. You know that child who's looking out from the school play or presentation and not seeing their parent in the audience? My parents never wanted me to be that child, and I don't feel like I ever was. They always made an effort. Of course, there were times when it got difficult, especially when he was running for vice president, but they made it a point to nurture kindness even in hectic times. They tried to be good to their kids and to one another. I try to follow my parents' example.
>
> HANI LIEBERMAN

Election Night was surreal. The results were coming in, but it was very confusing as to which states we had won. We were exhausted, tense. Gore conceded to Bush and then withdrew the concession. The numbers were too close to call. Eventually it became clear that the outcome of the election would hinge on ballots in three Florida counties: Broward, Dade, and Palm Beach. There was nothing to do but wait for the U.S. Supreme Court to weigh in. And wait. And wait. Many evenings we went out with the Gores, just to keep ourselves busy. Everywhere we went, people applauded and offered words of encouragement. They seemed to assume we knew more about what was going on than they did, which was not the case.

I was planning on it being just another Thanksgiving with our usual cast of characters, including, of course, Hadassah and Joe. Most of the family lived nearby and were able to go home at the end of the day, but Hadassah and Joe usually spent that night in our guest room. However, Thanksgiving 2000, like everything 2000, was different. The chads were still hanging, and Hadassah and Joe were still being protected by the United States Secret Service.

About a week before Thanksgiving, I received a call from an agent who said he was coming to my house to do an inspection. In fact, not just he but a number of agents, along with an adorable but very large bomb-sniffing German shepherd, came to check out our house, our yard, and the neighborhood. Among other goals, they needed to locate the best room in the house to set up their security office and settled on our master bedroom. I nixed that idea and offered the garage. Several days later, the agents returned to set up their "office," which involved running wires, setting up a high-security phone system, running checks on our list of attendees, and identifying possible security weaknesses.

Thanksgiving came, and the house smelled like . . . Thanksgiving. The aromas of roasting turkeys and baking apple pies permeated the air when, without warning, in walked several men accompanied by a profusely drooling German shepherd, torn between his duty to country and a nearly uncontrollable desire for turkey.

Before the day was over, I, in my very protected home, with help from my mother, prepared extra portions, which we served on table-clothed folding tables set up in our garage to the twenty or so agents who were missing their holiday so Joe could have his. We all took turns serving them, including Joe and Hadassah, and the agents were noticeably moved by their being respected and included in this way.

It was a very different and certainly memorable Thanksgiving

On Friday, December 9, in the late afternoon, we got some good news: the Florida Supreme Court had ordered a manual recount of ballots in the three contested counties. Al wanted Joe and me to be with him and Tipper that evening. Hani was with Joe's mother, so the two of us were driven, along with the Secret Service, to the Naval Observatory, the official residence of the vice president, along with our movable Shabbat feast. We brought the ritual objects used to welcome the Sabbath—candlesticks and candles, kiddush cup and wine, two challahs—and some food. Prior to dinner, Joe and I went into the living room to pray. When I was done, I noticed their lovely Christmas tree twinkling in the corner—talk about being inclusive! Tipper suggested that everyone put their BlackBerries away, in deference to us. It would be easy enough for someone to find us if necessary. Dinner was an intimate affair. Our conversation ranged broadly; we focused less on the election and more on the things for which we were grateful. At the end of the evening, the Gores walked us back to our house, trailed at a respectful distance by our Secret Service detail and their security vehicles.

The next day, we went to the synagogue for morning services as usual, still hopeful given this most recent turn of events. But by that afternoon, when we learned that the US Supreme Court had agreed to take the case, we were feeling much less optimistic. On the following Tuesday, the Supreme Court handed down its decision to overturn the Florida court's ruling requiring a manual recount in three counties. For the first time in the modern political era, the candidates who won the popular vote (by more than 500,000 ballots) did not win the majority of votes in the Electoral College. It was over. We'd lost to George Bush and Dick Cheney. We were all in shock. The next evening, Joe, Hani, and I were with the Gore family in Al's office in the Executive Office Building, when he conceded in a memorable speech. As you might imagine, it took us quite a while to process the news, though Joe did go back to work at the Senate the next morning. Ever my parents' daughter, I did my best to keep moving forward.

Since the Bush inauguration was at the Capitol on a Saturday, we initially thought we would avoid that long walk and stay at a nearby hotel on Friday night. Obviously, the hotel was crammed with excited Bush supporters so we decided, before Shabbat actually fell, to go back to our quiet house in Georgetown. The Weisels, our dear friends and neighbors, welcomed us into their home, as they had on many other occasions, for a lovely kosher Shabbat dinner. On our trek back to the Capitol the next morning, we passed many protesters who had been aligned with the Gore campaign. When they saw us, they were totally surprised and started cheering.

Later on Inauguration Day, coffee was being served by Tom Daschle, who was then Senate majority leader. It was a cold day, and Joe said he was going to get some coffee. As he ran to the designated room, he bumped into the newly sworn-in President George Bush for the first time. Bush said, "You made it a close race," to which Joe responded, "Any way I can support you, I will." And he remained true to his word.

NINE

Gratitude

Gratitude bestows reverence, allowing us to encounter everyday
epiphanies, those transcendent moments of awe that change
forever how we experience life and the world.

JOHN MILTON

After the election, I signed on with the Harry Walker Agency and began to give speeches across the country and abroad on the campaign, on women's health, and on my personal history as an immigrant and child of survivors. I loved the interaction with audience members and found that people connected with what I was saying. I had flown to Dallas to give such a speech on September 10, 2001. Little did I know what the next day would bring.

As Americans, we have certain tragedies embedded in our national consciousness. Time seems to stop as we collectively digest the news, mourn what has been lost, and then try to make sense of it before moving forward. For those who are affected most directly, this process can be long. Such memorable moments include the assassination of JFK, President Nixon resigning from office, the shooting of John Lennon, or the space shuttle *Challenger* disaster. On the morning of 9/11, I attended a Democratic breakfast fundraiser hosted by a charming real estate developer and philanthropist, Ray Nasher. Midway through the fundraiser, which was held around his large swimming pool, Nasher's daughter ran out, shouting and crying, "A plane has hit the World Trade Center."

Her words didn't register. But then we all went inside and watched in horror as the second plane struck. The shock was palpable. Something about our country had just fundamentally changed. We saw a vulnerability we had not experienced before. I wondered how my parents might have reacted to this—yet another unthinkable world event.

Taking a deep breath, I set myself in motion. My first thought was to call Joe and make sure he was safe and to check on Hani at school. Thankfully, the three older children were accounted for. Given his position, Joe would have a better sense of what was going on. While he was equally concerned about Hani, there was no way he could pick her up because he was at the Capitol. At that moment, there was extreme concern about what might occur in Washington as well as in New York. So much was still unknown, and we all hoped that nothing else would happen. When I was finally able to reach him, he told me that Lisa Leval, our close friend and neighbor, had picked up Hani as well as her own daughters. I was so grateful for her and for all my wonderful friends. I still am. It is never easy being a mother, or a wife, or maybe just a human being. But when you are in public service, there seem to be more pressures and responsibilities, and you are always going to have some conflicting feelings about what to prioritize in the moment. That's when we all really need each other.

Meanwhile, Heather Picazio, my trusted personal assistant and dear friend, was with me in Dallas and trying her best to get us home. We had gone back to our hotel to make arrangements, but every plane in the country was grounded. After two nights in Dallas, Heather was finally able to locate a car service to take us home. We packed our bags and headed to the hotel lobby. Just then a beat-up white sedan pulled up to the curb, and two men in T-shirts gestured for us to climb in. They certainly didn't look like professional drivers. Heather remembers that she was hesitant to get in the car with them. I must admit I was too. But then the reality of the moment hit me, and I knew, from someplace deep inside, that our commonality as Americans would shine through in this moment. I took my bags and got into the car.

The two men, Reggie and Kevin, bantered with each other as we drove to Washington but were polite yet distant with us. When we stopped at a diner, they headed to a different table. I wasn't surprised. After all, it had been apparent that we were initially afraid to get into the car with them. I knew that was wrong, especially in this moment. I invited them over to our table. Smiles broke across their faces as they sat down. My offer indicated, "We're in this together," and they understood. And so, in the most uncertain of times, I ate with strangers. They told me about their families, their lives, and their service in the military. By the time we got to Washington, I knew so much about them. In their words, I heard my own story. Over our twenty-five hours on the road together, we made a connection that represents to me what this country is all about.

When we arrived in Washington, the scope of what had happened became clearer. Sadly, the bubble of our car ride was broken. I had planned to give Reggie and Kevin a tour of the Capitol and Joe's office, but under the circumstances, that was impossible. They insisted on heading back to Texas, worried just like the rest of us.

Generally, I am not a fearful person. With the first death threat, I thought it was just an unbalanced individual. But things changed after 9/11. I had just run for vice president, and it was coming up to being near the High Holidays. Our dear buddy and unofficial security chief, Jimmy O'Connell, the man who drove us for thirty years, said that I should get protection from the Capitol Police for the Jewish holidays. They sent up a few guys who stayed with us for the holidays, and I thought that was the end of it. About two weeks later, we were having a vote on the Senate floor and the Sergeant-at-Arms, who is in charge of the Capitol Police, asked me how my security detail was going. "It was great," I said, telling him it had ended. "Senator," he said, shaking his head, "you just ran for vice president. We just had an Islamist terrorist attack on America. You are the most prominent Jewish American. You need a security detail full time. And besides, if something happens to you on my watch, it will be bad for my career. So I am ordering a security detail for you." That began a period of three years of having Capitol Police protection.

JOE LIEBERMAN

After the events of 9/11, we all adjusted to the new normal: the heightened security, the police protection, the less carefree existence. In 2003 and 2004, Joe sought the Democratic presidential nomination, and I was by his side, as ever, taking an active role in yet another campaign. Meanwhile, I continued the visits to my mother, whose condition was deteriorating. When she died in 2004, her caregivers from the Hebrew Home came to pay their respects, and we seated them in the front row during the funeral to acknowledge their kindness to her.

It's strange how life works. During Joe's presidential campaign, I happened to meet Nancy Brinker, the charismatic founder and CEO of the Susan G. Komen for the Cure Foundation. We discussed the launch of the foundation's Global Initiative, a project she was about to put into motion to expand breast cancer awareness around the world. Two years later, the foundation hired me in a consultant capacity as a global ambassador, working out of their DC office, and I continued in that role for the next six years, until 2012.

My focus was on raising international awareness of the realities of breast cancer. Whether launching a new project in Brazil or speaking with students in Saudi Arabia at a dental school for women or organizing events in Israel about how to recognize signs of breast cancer, I saw that we all had the same concerns. Working in international health felt right to me, as it combined two important policy tools: diplomacy and development. It allowed me to bring people together in new and exciting ways.

One of the projects I am especially proud of was helping to launch the first-ever Susan G. Komen Race for the Cure in Israel in 2012. It was extraordinary to walk through the streets of historic Jerusalem with Mayor Nir Barkat and women and men from around the world. There were Israelis, both religious and nonobservant; Druze Israelis; Arab Israelis; Americans visiting for the week or studying for the year; and immigrants to Israel from Russia, Ethiopia, France, and Iraq. Mayor Barkat was amazed. He told Nancy and me that he had never before seen such a diverse group of people marching together, united in their desire to help end breast cancer—a scourge that touches all our lives.

Joe, who had been on a Senate trip in the area, was able to join us for this unique and inspirational experience. We began at the Tower of David overlooking the walls of the Old City, which the Komen Foundation had lit with pink. Sara Netanyahu, wife of the prime minister, turned on lights that illuminated the entire city with the same hue. Fireworks exploded overhead that night, transmitting a pink glow over the horizon. On that day, I was reminded that whatever differences separate people, we are bound together by a common humanity. It moved and amazed me that thousands of eyes were focused on a single goal: curing breast cancer. For me, that's public service in its most heartwarming and indispensable form.

While my professional efforts helped to educate people about this disease, I didn't anticipate that I would benefit personally from my role. How ironic that one Sunday night while I was working for Komen, I discovered a lump in my breast. Like anyone else in this situation, I was terrified. The next morning, I went to see my doctor. He told me I would need to have a biopsy. My head felt fuzzy. Is this real or a nightmare? I was lucky that the disease was caught early—stage 1—though I needed surgery, chemotherapy, and radiation. The wonderful doctors at Georgetown Hospital scheduled my treatments for 7:00 a.m. so Joe could be there and then take me home before going to Capitol Hill. Sometimes I'd be in the midst of treatment and Joe's BlackBerry would start buzzing and he would have to step out of the room to take a call. Such is life.

I don't mean to minimize my experience; it was grueling. What helped me to get through it was the love and support of those closest to me, especially my husband, whose own strength, despite the difficulty of watching me go through the treatments, gave me strength. The doctors had warned that I might lose my hair, and I did. It may seem like a trivial thing to fixate on, but for so many women, hair is a significant part of our identity; without it, you may wonder if you are still *you*. When it was time to get a wig, Hani, who was living in New York City then but came to stay with us for an extended visit, insisted on going with me to make sure it was sufficiently flattering. When people complimented me on my new haircut, I would just nod and say, "Thank you."

I've never before discussed my illness publicly. I am an extremely private person, and I shared the devastating news with only family and a few close friends as I dealt with the treatments. But in writing this book, I feel I must articulate my experience in the hope that it may help someone else find the strength to speak out as they cope with their illness. As with divorce, every person's cancer journey is unique, but there are certain common experiences: the initial shock, the fear, the challenge of treatments, and the uncertainty that inevitably comes with the diagnosis. At times, what kept me going was the knowledge that I was not alone, that so many other women were also battling this disease. I realized we had to stand together and help each other be strong.

This commitment to doing work for the public good continues, as it does for Joe. After he left the Senate in 2013, he went back to practicing law and became chair of the No Labels initiative for more bipartisan, problem-solving government. In addition to giving occasional speeches, my professional endeavors largely revolve around volunteering for nonprofit organizations, including acting as a member of the UJA Federation of New York board of trustees. Though I support all of their activities, the ones that are closest to my heart include their outreach to the 40,000 Holocaust survivors living in the New York City area (40% of whom live in poverty), the development of kosher food pantries in the five boroughs, and the Marks Jewish Community House of Bensonhurst, which offers a broad range of services, including those designed specifically for Holocaust survivors, immigrants, and women and girls.

I would like to say that this time of my life is characterized by profound peace and quiet. However, that would be untrue. Although I no longer have a professional job, I am grateful for the many "jobs" I continue to have—as a mother, grandmother, friend, and the wife of an amazing man who, *Baruch Hashem*, still wants me by his side, publicly and privately.

While my own faith is based in traditional Judaism, I believe people of all religions have equally valid connections to G-d. For me, Judaism is a way to connect to my family and community. It offers a code to live by, a spiritual anchor in times of strife, and a system for creating a purposeful life. No matter what was happening in our lives, we always kept the Sabbath, a time when family can return to one another, to reset and focus on what is truly important. All of my children practice Judaism, each somewhat differently. I call us a rainbow coalition family. Hani often jokes that Joe and I think she is "too religious." Becca and I do not cover our hair, while

Hani does (it has been a longstanding custom for married women to cover their hair as a sign of modesty). All of our family go to synagogue on the holidays and the Sabbath, but some of us are more observant than others. All of our kitchens are kosher, following the set of dietary rules first delineated in the (Hebrew) Bible and subsequently interpreted and expanded on in the rabbinic tradition. My son Ethan often sets a vegetarian Shabbat table (I can't imagine what my mother would have said about that!) while the rest of us eat meat. But when we are gathered together on our day of rest, with nothing but *Hashem*, Shabbat, and each other on our minds and in our hearts, we are one.

My faith links me to my family's past and to a shared heritage. The world my parents lived through can seem at odds with the very G-d we worship. They were survivors of the worst tragedy known to humanity. When it ended, they could have become disillusioned and bitter. In fact, my father wrestled with many questions about G-d; nonetheless, he and my mother chose to embrace a religious path. While I had always known my father's commitment to Judaism was deep, I didn't fully appreciate the sacrifices he made for his religion until I read his memoir. I feel a duty to uphold the religion in which he sought refuge, even while being persecuted for it, and to pass our traditions onto my children and grandchildren.

We are such a short moment away from living in a world where all that will be left are children delivering hearsay testimony from their parents as to the reality of the Shoah. I grew up with my grandparents speaking about what they went through; all I have left now are my grandfather's book, my grandmother's pictures and my mother's second-order memories as opposed to my third-order ones.

Last night, on Holocaust Remembrance Day, my children came

home with candles that sit burning on our stove, each wrapped with the name of a victim of the Shoah. What struck me about this was not just having my children bear the names of individual victims but realizing that over a million Jewish children all over Israel were doing the same. And it seemed so simple to me at that moment: the trauma of the Shoah will ultimately fade when there are 6 million Jewish children, each able to kindle in their lives the light that was extinguished in one of their ancestors. This is the ultimate response. To build and to live. Perhaps it is best rendered in this context: vibrant, living human beings light G-d's way.

RABBI ETHAN TUCKER

My grandparents and my mother were in this reality of: "Why did we survive? Why were we not killed?" Clearly what they experienced affected me tremendously.

I remember one time when I was looking at photos from the Holocaust in a book. My grandmother took the book from me because there was a picture of a large group of rescued camp survivors who all looked weak and sick. She took it and said, "Let me look at this. Is my mother in here?"

A lot of the pain I think both my grandparents and mother felt translated to a connection to Israel. That's the next step in terms of my religious observance, my connection to Israel, and my wanting to raise my children there. It's something I can do that's proactive and productive.

HANI LIEBERMAN

Of course, we all face challenges. In this book, I've discussed some of mine, including my illness and coping with divorce. Then there were the many political campaigns that tested my stamina, as well as my ability to maintain some semblance of a private life in the midst of very public events. And yet I remain grateful for all that I've been given. As I reflect on my life, I recognize how deeply I was shaped by the immigrant experience. Coming to this country, my family was greeted by Emma Lazarus's words at the Statue of Liberty, words that my mother especially held dear and invoked frequently with gratitude. We believed those words, just like we believed in this country that accepted us as we were. Being an immigrant has made me appreciate more fully the strangers in our midst and the necessity of opening our hearts to them.

Fixed in my memory is my father's oft-told story of how, after World War II, a group of rabbis went to England in an attempt to find some of the Jewish children who had been sent there during the war to be raised by kind strangers. According to my father, the rabbis would start reciting the Sh'ma—an essential Jewish prayer, known by even those whose connection to the religion may have grown quite tenuous—in order to determine the young person's heritage. If the children joined the rabbi in reciting the prayer, it was clear they had started their childhood in a Jewish home. How could you not embrace such a child who has lost so much? Similarly, how can we not welcome the immigrants in our midst?

We have entered a dark period in our history. Given the alarming presence of hate speech today, it may seem hard to believe that over the course of the 2000 campaign, we *never* encountered any anti-Semitic behavior or remarks. In fact, we were embraced by people of various religions and backgrounds. What a far cry from the present, when it seems as if the very air is full of hateful images and words, directed at anyone who is "different," and transmitted by television, radio, in print, and via the Internet. I find it shocking and unsettling. The need to regulate the Internet in some way is a topic for another book and a challenge to anyone who believes, as I do, in freedom of speech. Yet I would be remiss if I did not acknowledge the role it has played in allowing hate and misinformation to fester.

My hope is that we can counter this darkness with more light, more love, more transparency and honesty.

Reflecting on the subtitle of this book, *An American Story*, I think of immigration in two ways. There is the usual definition: "A person from one country who comes to another country to take up permanent residence there in the hope of having a better life." But there is another description, one that characterizes immigrants as "people who become established in an area where they were previously unknown."

My life has been informed by my quest to establish a distinct identity as Hadassah Freilich, as Hadassah Lieberman, and as just plain Hadassah so that I can make a difference in "places where I was previously unknown."

I hope that some of the things I have shared in these pages will be helpful to you.

Afterword

My father, John McCain, and Joe Lieberman were longtime friends and colleagues in the Senate. During the difficult period of my father's illness, the Liebermans would come to visit him at his ranch while I was also there.

I knew my father and Joe were close, but I did not know much about Hadassah's background as an immigrant until these visits. Hearing about her family's experiences, so different from my own, and then reading this book moved me. Both of her parents were survivors—her mother of concentration camps, her father of a slave labor camp—who then made the journey to America and were embraced by the inhabitants of a small town in New England. It makes me so proud as an American to hear stories like this.

In Joe's eulogy for my father, he remarked, "The greater cause to which [my father] devoted his life was America, not so much the country defined by its borders, but the America of our founding values, freedom, human rights, opportunity, democracy, and equal justice under the law." These are the values that enabled a young immigrant girl to travel from Gardner, Massachusetts, to the halls of power in Washington, DC. I hope that as a nation, we will continue to uphold these values and open our arms to newcomers in this way. *Hadassah* is a poignant reminder of what our country can be.

Meghan McCain

HBI SERIES ON JEWISH WOMEN

Sylvia Barack Fishman | General Editor

Lisa Fishbayn Joffe | Associate Editor

The HBI Series on Jewish Women, created by the Hadassah-Brandeis Institute, publishes a wide range of books by and about Jewish women in diverse contexts and time periods. Of interest to scholars and the educated public, the HBI Series on Jewish Women fills major gaps in Jewish Studies and in Women and Gender Studies as well as their intersection.

The HBI Series on Jewish Women is supported by a generous gift from Dr. Laura S. Schor.

For the complete list of books that are available in this series, please see https://www.brandeis.edu/press/books/series.html.

BRANDEIS SERIES IN AMERICAN JEWISH HISTORY, CULTURE, AND LIFE

Jonathan D. Sarna | Editor

Sylvia Barack Fishman | Associate Editor

This series encompasses all areas of American Jewish civilization, including history, religion, thought, politics, economics, sociology, anthropology, literature, and the arts. The series emphasizes contemporary and interdisciplinary studies, and volumes that tie together divergent aspects of the American Jewish experience.

For a complete list of books that are available in this series, please see https://www.brandeis.edu/press/books/series.html.